the 90-day play

by
Linda Walsh Jenkins

the
90-day
novel®
press

COPYRIGHT 2017
A publication of The 90-Day Novel Press

the
90-day
novel
press

A publication of The 90-Day Novel Press.
ISBN 978-0-9831412-6-6

TABLE OF CONTENTS

PART ONE

PART TWO

UNIT ONE:
IMAGINING, COLLECTING, AND PLANNING

WEEK 1: Inventing Your Dramatic World

WEEK 2: Creating Character Dimensions

UNIT TWO:
WRITING THE BEGINNING

UNIT THREE:
MOVING THROUGH THE MIDDLE

UNIT FOUR:
DRIVING TO THE END

PART THREE

PART FOUR

PART FIVE

PART SIX

INTRODUCTION

Y ou want to write a play but don't know how to go about it. Perhaps you began once but couldn't finish. Or you've written a play or two but would like guidance. You might be a screenwriter or a novelist who wants to learn more about the nature of drama. I've designed *The 90-Day Play* for students and teachers, writing partners, and the individual writing alone in her room with no one to turn to for advice and support. Beginners can use the book daily to imagine and construct a play. More experienced writers will find exercises, examples from plays, and examinations of structure and technique to add to their toolboxes.

The 90-Day Play is not only for the protagonist-driven drama. Whether a theatrical event is realistically staged in what appears to be real time, a Brechtian ensemble drama, or a surrealistic time-bending fantasy, writers generate "What will happen next?" curiosity in an audience. If you are creating a one-person show you are weaving a theatrical experience with a beginning, middle, and end. Playwrights make decisions about characters, themes, theatricality, structure, and language. The 90-Day process can help you create intrigue while activating your imagination and designing a satisfying structure.

Drama shows humans in turmoil, faced with choices, resisting or embracing change, confronting confounding situations. Plays invite us to view ourselves and our society truthfully, whether through realism or theatre of the absurd or farce. As you write you will question and wrestle with beliefs, attitudes, biases, and perceptions. You will use characters' arguments and action to experiment with those beliefs.

I've worked with new plays and playwrights as a teacher, dramaturge and actress in Minneapolis, Chicago, and Los Angeles. As an associate professor at Northwestern University I focused on the architecture of drama from its Greek roots into the present. Former students and colleagues have won major playwriting awards including the Pulitzer, Tony,

MacArthur, and other honors in the US and internationally. Others direct and produce new plays at theatres throughout the country. With this book I share what I've learned through these experiences about helping an idea grow organically into its appropriate form, flexibility with and respect for formal principles, and techniques to nourish inspiration.

Linda Walsh Jenkins
Fort Worth, Texas

WHY THE 90-DAY PROCESS?

The 90-Day Process is about bypassing our internal critic and getting the first draft down quickly. I always tell my students that what is impossible to achieve in ten years becomes possible in ninety days. Once we've done the heavy lifting of developing a relationship to the characters and their world, we want to let go of our idea of how the story should unfold in order to let the characters live. Our subconscious is the seat of our genius. It makes connections and constructs patterns that we may only become conscious of in retrospect. Ninety days gives us enough time to fill the pages but not so much time that we get into our heads and kill the aliveness of our story. Our brains tend to seek solutions through logic, yet there is nothing logical about human nature. We humans are a hornet's nest of contradictions and when we attempt to codify our characters' behavior, our work tends to suffer. The first draft is where we take risks and surprise ourselves; and in the rewrite we can approach our work in a more analytical way.

In his book, *The Seven Habits of Highly Effective People,* Steven Covey talks about the importance of beginning with the end in mind. By having a clearly defined deadline, a shift occurs in our subconscious. We recognize the impossibility of completing the task *perfectly* and the psychic burden of creating a result is lifted. When we give ourselves unlimited time we actually put more pressure on ourselves because the stakes are heightened.

I first heard about Linda Jenkins from one of her former students who studied playwriting with her at Northwestern University. Her approach to playwriting was very much in sync with the process I teach at L.A. Writers' Lab, and after a number of discussions, I knew she was the right person to write this book.

The 90-Day Play is the fourth book in the L.A. Writers' Lab series. Linda Jenkin's workbook is not only instructive but also intuitive. It was created in concert with her teaching the workshop and is both a workbook and a response to the playwright's questions and concerns. By letting go of our idea of how the story should go, we are set free to let the work become what it was always meant to be.

ALAN WATT
Los Angeles, California

the 90-day play

B efore you begin writing, review the overall plan of the process you'll follow as well as definitions of common dramatic terms. Prepare for the adventure ahead with practical guidelines. If you are a teacher, consider suggestions for the book's use in your classroom.

AN OVERVIEW OF THE PROCESS

T he *90-Day Play* will guide you day-by-day through writing a first draft of a scripted full-length play of approximately 80-120 pages, and provide suggestions for revision. You can adapt the daily lessons to a shorter play. I include examples from a broad range of plays as well as exercises or suggestions pertinent to each daily lesson.

I suggest you begin with a passion for an idea/story/theme and discover what form that should take. The discovery of form is in itself a primary element of the creative process. Your play might be the enactment of a story, the illumination of a theme through a collection of interviews or a collage of scenes illustrating the human condition. You might call for the illusion of "reality" with a "fourth wall" or engage the audience through direct address. The process in this book can be adapted to the form you choose.

By dividing your project into Imagining and Collecting, Beginning, Middle, and End you'll find the prospect of writing a play realistic and manageable. In the first twenty-eight day unit, you will develop ideas and characters with exercises and by collecting thoughts through stream-of-consciousness. You don't start drafting the play from beginning to end during these early weeks, though you probably will sketch scenes, dialogues and monologues. Give yourself time to experiment with possibilities while the play emerges in this fashion. Having decided on a likely scenario by the end of the first unit, you will begin writing the play. That scenario will be sketchy and flexible. I will guide you from Beginning through Middle and to the End of this first draft in the three units that follow.

If possible, you will write every day for 90 Days, two hours per day. However, you can adjust this schedule to suit your life's demands; for example, perhaps you'll write three or five days a week. You can finish a draft if you are disciplined and meet deadlines.

While creating the first draft you will learn about the play's potential. Rarely does a writer fully grasp his or her idea until s/he plunges in and wrestles it through to the end. I'll give you advice for rewriting as well as for readings and workshops in Part Three. You probably will write many drafts before you have fully plumbed the possibilities and shaped the play.

Relax, free your imagination and enjoy this process with the goal of learning, not perfection.

PREPARATION

Before you begin writing day by day, prepare for the process.

- Decide how much time (preferably two hours) you will set aside to write and where you will create. Make your play a top priority.
- Hold your ideas for the play loosely at this point. You might find it easiest to carry a main character through a dramatic experience in a simple setting without a large cast, using a tight time frame. But if that won't work for your idea, let your imagination be your guide.
- Avoid talking about your play to others. Let the story grow and change within you. Responses by others might lead you astray or give you doubts while ideas incubate.
- If you don't have a practical grasp of theatre, you can benefit from reading an introductory text. See the Bibliography at the end of this book.
- Don't write what you think "the market" wants.
- Consider how plays influence people—what characters learn (or don't), what we learn from reading and watching, what a production ensemble learns.
- You are creating something for other artists to bring into being for audiences. You cannot fully control how people will interpret or respond.
- If you are fearful or insecure at the outset of this process, relax and focus on your ideas. This first draft is for you only; it can't be "wrong" or "not good enough" because simply by completing it you will succeed.

GENERATING IDEAS

If you don't yet have an idea for a play, these suggestions might help:

Familiar situations and conflicts — Consider a situation such as people dealing with a death, weddings, reunions, holidays, and so forth. Ground a story in conflicts familiar to you such as jealousy, betrayal, old wounds, misunderstandings, family crises.

Existing stories — You don't have to imagine an original story. That wasn't a problem for Sophocles or Racine or Shakespeare, or for that matter Adrienne Kennedy or Charles Mee. Play imaginatively with an existing story.

News — Often police, legal and medical procedurals start with something that actually happened. They change names and details and "open up" the story for the sake of drama and efficiency. David Henry Hwang was inspired by a news article to write *M. Butterfly*, which varies greatly from its source.

History — Adaptation from a published source, like a biography of George Washington, usually requires legal permission to produce or publish. However, if you do your own research with multiple sources and do not plagiarize, you might not violate an author's legal protections. You can't use another writer's words verbatim, but you can use George Washington's.

Adaptations of familiar stories and myths — No one needs permission to write a version of Sleeping Beauty or Jack in the Beanstalk or Oedipus or Medea.

Adaptations of published material (plays, novels, stories, films, etc.) — If you are writing only to learn the process, with no intention of attempting to produce or publish, you can use anything already written as a basis for your play. However, you would have to obtain legal permission for anything but your own personal enjoyment. If you can translate a play written long ago from the original, you probably will not violate legal rights; but if you adapt from a single translation you could need permission from the publisher unless you're doing this only for the exercise.

You can adapt a very old play in English, like Shakespeare's plays, with no legal problems.

You might examine plays adapted from published sources such as Jessica Hagedorn's stage version of her own novel, *Dogeaters*. Look for acting editions of adaptations of novels by Charles Dickens and Jane Austen, as well as Sarah Ruhl's "take" on Virginia Woolf's *Orlando*. Study Robert Breen's advice in *Chamber Theatre*.

The advantage of adaptation is that characters, dramatic world, plot points, themes, and language have been invented by the author. You must selectively and imaginatively find a visual life, edit some characters and subplots, discover theatrical efficiency, and invent new elements to effect the transition from one form into another.

Interviews, letters, other materials — As with adaptations, you can create dramatic arrangements of nondramatic material for your own purposes but should seek legal advice if you intend production or publication. You could collect interviews or written materials from a group of people in response to questions you ask—like Anna Deveare Smith does in *Twilight: Los Angeles, 1992*. Please get permission from people who contribute to use their comments as well as refer to them.

KEEP PERSONAL AND PLAY JOURNALS

Keep one journal to chronicle personal thoughts and the other to collect ideas about your play. They can be in separate sections of the same notebook, separate computer files, different notebooks, or whatever works for you. Both journals will contribute to more efficient first drafts and better rewrites. Writing down your thoughts, instead of keeping them in your head, can help clarify and "empty" your mind to better achieve "flow."

Personal journal — Notice what's in your imagination at the end of writing sessions, at moments during the day, before sleep, and first thing in the morning. This will help you learn to be objective and descriptive about what you've written, your habits and how you write. Use this journal to discover a process that works for you.

Play journal — Record observations about the play itself (puzzles, questions, thoughts, notes to self and exercises).

- Use this journal to collect and plan without self-censorship.
- Allow yourself to write in stream-of-consciousness.
- Don't force an organization of your thoughts, but if you can identify a category or structure for them, do so.

Keep at least some of your notes in longhand if possible; you may find that you think differently in longhand than on the computer. Also, it's easier to make notes in longhand anywhere you go. A small notebook, smartphone or other portable computing device might work for you to take notes when you aren't at home.

INTRODUCTION TO TERMS

Throughout the 90-Day course I'll repeat and review these and additional terms in more detail, with many exercises and ample examples from plays. (Please see the Index at the end of the book for the scope of this terminology.)

- *Drama/Action/Conflict* — Drama results from characters' internal and external behavior, not the "act" of running or pouring water. For the Greek writers, "drama" and "action" (*agon*) carried the same meaning. People make choices and take actions for motivations known and unknown, with reactions and consequences that drive towards a conclusion.

- *Drama/Theatre* — Often "drama" and "theatre" are used interchangeably. Typically "drama" refers to the action of the play (conflicts and events). Drama can occur in television, film and novels as well. Comedies are dramatic. A theatre is by definition a "seeing place." When we talk about "theatre," we mean a live performance event. In a theatre we experience a drama. You are writing a drama for the theatre.

- *Story* — The story is the overall complex of characters, events, and themes that generates your play, including events well before the action onstage begins. The story of Cinderella, for example, begins before her father marries the wicked stepmother and continues after she marries the Prince.

- *Plot* — The plot is the accumulation of events and information from that story (each event is a *plot point*) that are germane to your play.

- *Scenario* — In your scenario you arrange the plot points in order as they will be staged moment to moment. The same plot might be arranged in various ways. It can go backwards in time or incorporate flashbacks. In one arrangement an event could happen onstage, while in another arrangement it occurs offstage. One of the most important choices you will make is the arrangement of the plot points.

    Your scenario will generate suspense as characters are in conflict, as they confront obstacles and contradictions, and if they turn to allies. You might employ misdirection, teasers, cliffhangers and "forwards," setups, inciting incidents, character expansions, the contraction of plot points as crisis approaches, and reversals of expectation for the audience and for main character(s). Consider what's at stake and the emotional outcomes for as many characters as possible as the action peaks.

If you aren't writing a conventionally structured play, you will choose events to stage and make decisions about how to arrange them. You might organize events by theme or another principle. You will make something happen on stage and those plot points have to be arranged in a deliberate manner (scenario) to achieve an emotional and aesthetic dramatic goal.

- *Protagonist* — Most plays are anchored by a main character that either drives the action or centers it and is driven by it. We call that person the protagonist from the Greek for "first actor." Not every play has one protagonist. Sometimes an ensemble is the anchor.

- *Antagonist* — An antagonist, or "second actor," thwarts the main protagonist or prods the protagonist into action. You might create more than one antagonist.

- *Language* — "Language" means vocabulary, characters' styles, diction, slang, rhythms, dialects, use of figurative speech, text vs. subtext, monologues, dialogue, song, stories told within scenes, silences within scenes.

- *Theatricality* — "Theatricality" refers to how a play is shown visually as well as the use of sound and special effects.

- *Theme* — Themes are the ideas your play illuminates about humans. Often a writer discovers theme(s) while creating a play. Remain open to discovery.

- *Style* — Your play and its style are extensions of you. You seek to create consistency and congruency in the combination of elements. Also, think of the play's style as it might fit within a category such as comedy of manners, tragedy, and so forth.

- *Tragedy/Dramedy* — Tragedies and dramedies give serious treatment to serious matters. A tragedy usually blows open a dramatic world, throwing that world off balance in order to expose and possibly heal but lay bare uncomfortable truths with serious consequences for characters. "Dramedy" is a fairly new term, usually meaning a serious action with ample humor that doesn't end in outright catastrophes or deaths. *Hamlet* is a tragedy. *Who's Afraid of Virginia Woolf?* might be termed a dramedy.

- *Comedy* — A comedy shows up human foolishness (societal, situational, current fashions, character traits) to delight an audience. It can expose serious issues but ultimately comedy punctures conceit and resolves with normalcy. The many variations of comedy include but are not limited to parody, satire, farce, and slapstick. It requires an oral and physical instinct, which can and should be honed, for timing, setups, teases, shaping, and punchlines. If you are writing a comedy, see the Bibliography at the end of this book for some useful guides.

- *Melodrama* — In the 19th century, Western theatre melodramas were big spectacles with musical accompaniment and simple character types, little nuance, and heavy sentimentality celebrating the triumph of good over evil. Now the term usually indicates a play in which characters serve the plot more than vice versa and in which characters don't learn or change so much as grapple with obstacles.

- *Epic/Brechtian Theatre* — Erwin Piscator and later Bertold Brecht introduced a form that has been called "epic" or "Brechtian." Believing that audiences were easily lulled by plays that invite sentiment, these German theatre pioneers created plays that interrupt dramatic stories with various methods—direct address, film, didactic songs—to dispel illusion and challenge people to think rationally about social and political issues.

- *Fourth Wall* — Often actors/characters pretend they don't know we're watching, as if there is a "wall" between us and them. There's a real wall behind them onstage, and usually there are walls to either side of them. The "fourth wall" is the imaginary one.

- *Direct Address* — This term refers to when an actor/character "breaks" the fourth wall and speaks directly to the audience.

- *Stage Directions* — If you are an actor onstage, behind you is "upstage," the direction towards the audience is "downstage," to your right is "stage right" and to your left is "stage left." "Center stage" is in the center. It's possible to be "upstage center" and so forth. Conversely, if you are seated in the audience, the area to your right is "audience right" and the area to your left is "audience left."

- *Suspension of Disbelief* — When the audience enters into "play" with a theatre event, they suspend ordinary belief and accept the play's logic. We agree to suspend disbelief while a little boy flies through a window, ghosts appear, characters share their inner thoughts, and time flies across decades and continents.

STREAM-OF-CONSCIOUSNESS PRACTICE EXERCISES

Practice letting your writing flow with "stream-of-consciousness" as you collect and invent for your play. Let your thoughts flow like water. If a river bumps up against a mountain, it turns to flow around it. If dammed, the river rises and flows outward. The water doesn't stop moving as it adjusts to circumstances. For the process of collecting and writing exercises, let your mind flow with the first words and ideas that come to you. Relax your censoring mind and discover the abundance of your imagination. You can write in sentence fragments or single words, whatever comes to your mind as it occurs to you without censorship, like a runaway train. This is not about creating pretty prose or linear coherence. The more you practice writing in stream-of-consciousness using your own true "voice," the easier ideas will emerge. As you become adept at this process you can achieve more in your writing sessions.

To "warm up" before you begin your disciplined 90 Days, write for at least five minutes on the following topics or "prompts." Set a timer and write as quickly as you can. Don't think. Just write. Don't stop at five minutes if you're "flowing" and enjoying yourself. These are for your use only, so don't place boundaries on what you write. If you think of more topics along these lines, write about them as well.

For your Personal Journal:
　　1. I want to write for a theatre audience because . . .
　　2. These are some of my favorite moments from plays and why:
　　3. These are some of my least favorite theatrical plot devices:
　　4. These are questions and concerns I have about writing a play:
　　5. These are strengths and flaws I observe in people I know well:
　　6. These are strengths and flaws I observe in myself:
　　7. This is how I see the difference between "real" people and characters in plays:
　　8. These are the rules I give myself for writing this play:

For your Play Journal:
From the point of view and in the voice of any character (or more than one) you have in mind for your play, complete the following statements:
　　1. One thing you should know about me is . . .

2. The thought that keeps me up at night is . . .

3. I feel trapped when . . .

4. The bravest thing I've ever done is . . .

5. The most cowardly thing I've ever done is . . .

Stay open to possibilities, be patient, be disciplined, and have fun writing a play.

SUGGESTIONS
FOR THE CLASSROOM

Playwriting is a dynamic form of learning about theatre and drama because it requires consideration and integration of all the components of stagecraft. A writer must engage his/her whole self— intellect, creativity, feelings, personality, observations of self and others, imagination for multi-dimensional scenes, and deeply held beliefs. While some teachers introduce playwriting late in a student's theatre education, others might consider this as an effective introduction to the art and craft of the stage.

The 90-Day Play's organization of process, exercises, examples, and descriptions of terms and principles can aid lesson planning. Whether you have ten weeks or thirty, the basic format of the book is flexible. Daily letters and exercises might be assigned for reading, discussion, and exams. I suggest the following for assignments:

- Long play: 1/3 planning, 2/3 drafting (further broken into working on the Beginning, Middle, and End)
- Short play: 1/3 planning, 1/3 draft, 1/3 rewrite

If students don't come into a class with ideas for plays, suggestions in Part One/Preparation should help generate ideas.

At the end of this book are suggested readings in plays and books about theatre. In daily letters I refer to many plays as examples of the building blocks of drama. Most students study plays thematically or study characters (or both) but rarely examine how plays are constructed.

GUIDING DISCUSSIONS

Critiquing new work is challenging, especially with beginning writers. See Part Five: Rewriting, Readings, Submission and Production. Focus discussion on the strongest aspect of the material read aloud or circulated for reading. The more writers can understand their strengths, the better they can figure out their personal styles and be encouraged to keep writing. We are all very hard on ourselves; often we doubt others will like anything we've written.

Ask questions about the logic and consistency of plot, character or style if you find that confusing. "Why did Darcy pick up the flute when in the scene before he said he was a drummer?" Let the writer note the question without having to defend or explain.

You might provide students with "comment forms" on which they write questions and make respectful observations which they hand to the teacher. The teacher sorts through those and decides which to pass on to the writer, and how to do so.

PART TWO

the 90-day play

UNIT ONE

IMAGINING, COLLECTING AND PLANNING

In the first twenty-eight days you will focus on imagining characters, the world they inhabit, the setting, possible dramatic actions and clashes, possible beginnings and endings, the sound and look of the play, the shapes of dramatic action, and how your play will interact with your audience. In Unit Two you will begin to create the play from the first moment.

WEEK 1

INVENTING YOUR DRAMATIC WORLD

During these seven days you will invent ideas and images for your characters and their dramatic world through stream-of-consciousness exercises without concern for structure. You will discover and collect possibilities for the play while freeing your subconscious.

DAY 1

*"Work hard, do the best you can, don't ever lose faith
in yourself and take no notice of what other people say
about you."*

—NOEL COWARD

ENTERING PLAY TIME

Hi Writers,

As you reflect on the idea you have for a play you might find your mind flooded with images and small fragments of dialogue or action. You fear you don't know how to organize them. For now you do not need to impose order. Appreciate the wildness of imagination and simply collect those images and fragments as they come to you. You are creating something very real out of the substance of your imagination, memories and observations, personality and passions. By playing with ideas freely from the outset you can enrich imagination and passion.

Let your characters inhabit their dramatic world as fully as possible so that audiences can enjoy the adventures there. Even if the setting for your play is a living room, there is a house beyond those walls, and a neighborhood beyond that. Some people influence your characters that never appear onstage. A character's past and the future s/he longs for or fears are a part of that world. Now is the time for you to envision the larger context in which eventually you will craft a very specific drama. You won't know for a while what really belongs in the play or what merely helps you create this world but won't appear in the draft. You create the rules, the logic, the way people speak. Play "what if" with characters and situations; turn them upside down and inside out.

Feel free to write scenes and dialogue that occur to you. Instead of thinking of them as "scene one" or "end of play," give them titles that refer to what is happening in the scene: "Larry begs Eric to forgive him," "Sue discovers the lie," and so forth. This allows freedom to move the order around.

There is no one "right way" to begin working on your idea and your characters. Some people begin with a sketchy "big picture" and shadowy figures, moving from that "macro" view into "micro" specifics. Others start very close to characters and relationships, unsure where the story will take them. It doesn't matter where or how you begin, just write. Investigate, probe, make discoveries, flesh out what is at first skeletal.

If you're composing scenes, dialogues, monologues, and/or staging ideas on a computer before you begin drafting the play, I suggest you use professional script formatting now so you won't waste time reformatting later. This way you can cut and paste material you want to use as you write the script. Some people use format software such as Final Draft. (See Day 27 for an example of formatting and Part Six for a compilation of formatting suggestions.) Standard formatting helps a reader shift from one kind of description to another and follow characters' speeches. You might choose a variation on these standards, but be consistent.

WRITING EXERCISES FOR TODAY:

For these and all exercises I give you, commit to writing for at least five minutes each. Set a timer if that will help. Continue writing without a time limit if you are inspired to do so.

1. Spill out in stream-of-consciousness all the current ideas you have for the play with no censoring, no editing. You can write in sentence fragments and single words.
2. What makes you express your ideas through a play instead of a novel or screenplay?
3. What do you want to figure out, to investigate, by writing this play?
4. What are your feelings as you begin this adventure?

Until tomorrow,
Linda

HOMEWORK FOR THE WEEK

Cover as many daily exercises as possible during your writing time. However, don't artificially stop a flow of good ideas simply to attempt another exercise. How to use writing time will vary by the person and the project. Some of your "writing" time will be "thinking" time. The more deeply you delve into your idea, characters, composition, conflicts, themes, and so forth, the more you will fill your time with useful discoveries.

1. Do the daily writing exercises.

2. Continue imagining and exploring your dramatic world and characters without self-censoring.

3. If you have time and/or lack inspiration, play with the stream-of-consciousness exercises at the end of this book, concentrating on characters.

4. Write in your personal journal what you observe about your process, doubts, and habits.

DAY 2

"[Ideas] don't come ready formed. . . . On the contrary, they come as scruffy disjointed fragments, their potential barely visible."

—**ALAN AYCKBOURN**

PLACING THE ACTION

Hi Writers,

Today we concentrate on where you set your action—not the scenery, but the fictional place where the drama will occur. Envision all the possible places for your drama now without feeling pressure to make decisions. The setting(s) you choose for the action affect audiences and characters. Investigate what those effects might be.

Whether your dramatic world is as "realistic" as *Long Day's Journey into Night,* as meta-theatrical as *The Skin of Our Teeth,* or like Sam Shepard's *The Tooth of Crime* in which science-fiction meets rock and roll, there is an integral relationship between characters and their world. You invent place, time, event, situation, and other "rules of the game."

A play can be set in a very specific place like River City, Iowa, in *The Music Man* that nevertheless "stands for" other small American towns. It can be set in a king's palace or in a diner along a bus route. George and Martha control the drama in *Who's Afraid of Virginia Woolf?* by hosting a hapless young couple in their home.

The place can be suggestive: Vladimir and Estragon are on a country road by a tree in *Waiting for Godot*; the setting suggests journey, real and figurative, which is at the heart of the play's themes. "The scene is a New York subway is the Tower of London is a Harlem hotel room is St. Peter's" in Adrienne Kennedy's *The Owl Answers.* The action shifts as if through subway stops in this non-realistic meditation on the relationship of site to identity and culture.

WRITING EXERCISES FOR TODAY:

1. Where might the play take place? Why this place or these places for dramatic reasons?
2. What about this place (these places) can be entertaining for an audience?
3. Why do you like this choice of place? Does it have special meaning for you?
4. What are the theatrical limitations to your ideas for place?
5. Are characters meeting in a place that's familiar to all of them or to just a few? What difference does the familiarity or the strangeness make to each of them? Write a monologue for each character describing their reactions.
6. Do any characters have memories of this place? Good? Bad? Embarrassing? Write a monologue for each character describing that memory.
7. What difference does the place make to the characters' interactions?

Until tomorrow,
Linda

DAY 3

"The ability of writers to imagine what is not the self, to familiarize the strange and mystify the familiar, is the test of their power."

—**TONI MORRISON**

THE WHEN AND WHY OF IT

Hi Writers,

Your characters meet in a particular place at a certain *time* for a reason. The time of your action should have dramatic and thematic significance for other people, not just for you. The action might occur at a battleground during the Civil War while officers plot a surprise attack. The time might be a specific date and year or more generally a certain decade. It could be a week before or after a major catastrophe. Tony Kushner's *A Bright Room Called Day* juxtaposes building tensions in anti-semitic 1930s Germany against the early years of AIDS in 1980s America. The ancient Greek plays are set in "mythic" time in which themes, not clock time, matter.

There is a close relationship between the time of the drama and the *event* or events where your characters interact. For dramatic purposes, there should be a compelling reason for these characters to be here at this time; they want to be here, or they're forced to do so. And there's a reason some stay when conflict occurs. Decide what brings your characters together, what makes them stay, and why that would be interesting for an audience.

In *Ma Rainey's Black Bottom*, August Wilson assembles black and white characters in a Chicago recording studio in the 1920s. They clash across generations and races, exposing power dynamics within African-American culture as well as between the races. It would be almost impossible to construct the tensions and theatricality of that drama by placing the same characters in a living room with no special event or cultural context to gather them.

Also, note that the *time pressures* of the recording studio constrict *Ma Rainey's* action. This device is called "the ticking clock." In *'night, Mother* a woman tells her mother that she's going to kill herself very soon. *Dinner at Eight* takes us through various problems and choices people must make before a crucial dinner party. With a deadline that forces people to act—whether that's a bomb about to blow up or a wedding due to begin—you give characters more dramatic opportunities and create suspense.

WRITING EXERCISES FOR TODAY:

1. What time might be the setting for the play (now, another decade?) Why this time or these times for dramatic and entertaining reasons?
2. Do time pressures affect your characters and create tension? How?
3. Is something special happening that brings your characters together (for example, a wedding, a funeral, election, party, weekend in the country)? Why will that be dramatic?
4. What is it about this event that's different from the familiar and unpredictable?
5. What does this event mean to each character?

Until tomorrow,
Linda

DAY 4

*"Rarely when a play comes to me do I know how I will
develop it. . . . It comes out drop by drop, as I let [the
characters] sink into my thoughts."*

—NEIL SIMON

INHABITING YOUR CHARACTERS

Hi Writers,

When you invent the details of the world you are discovering characters.
Before deciding what shape you'll give to your characters' actions, inhabit them—discover their inner tensions, contradictions, and imbalances.
In *How to Read Literature*, Terry Eagleton surveys many ways in which
the idea of a "character" has varied across cultures and time; this history
might help you reflect on what a "character" is to you and how that informs your writing. What kinds of characters are you creating and why?
Are they like familiar "types" or are they unique to an extreme? Are they
based on people you know or read about?

Everyone onstage is a character. If your play's structure and style is
not realistic and the focus is more on theme and situation than natural-
istic characters (like Vladimir and Estragon in Samuel Beckett's *Waiting
for Godot*), the 90-Day exercises will help you explore those characters.
Even when actors are "playing themselves" as they do in Peter Handke's
Offending the Audience, the actors are characters whose words and actions
are selected for theatrical as well as dramatic effect.

August Wilson took his cues from the blues, which gave him "a world
that contained my image." His plays vivify "a nonliterate people whose history and culture were rooted in the oral tradition." Both the blues and the
people who sang them, who lived their stories, gave Wilson a dramatic
world for the characters in plays such as *Ma Rainey's Black Bottom* and *Joe
Turner's Come and Gone*. Perhaps such a world has shaped your characters'
inner lives—a small town, an urban subculture, a work environment.

You will begin to see and hear your characters all around you—in the
news, in conversations, in your relationships and observed relationships,

in your readings and music. The process of writing a play can help you pay better attention to your environment, and in turn your present reality can assist you in creating the dramatic world that will constitute your play.

WRITING EXERCISES FOR TODAY:

Answer the following questions for each character in your play.

1. What from the past haunts this character? Let the character speak about it in monologue.
2. Is there a tension or an unusual contrast between the character's work life and inner life (like a soldier/poet)? Have the character talk about his/her work and that contrast.
3. What makes your character angry and why? Write an angry monologue for each character.
4. How does your character behave when s/he's angry? Describe that behavior in detail.

Until tomorrow,
Linda

DAY 5

> ROTHKO: *"We exist—all of us, for all time—in a state of perpetual dissonance."*
>
> —**JOHN LOGAN's** *Red*

DISSONANCE

Hi Writers,

Dissonance is "a harsh, discordant combination of sounds; a state of disagreement or conflict." Dissonance within, between, and among characters constitutes the "action" of the play. This is true regardless of your play's structure or style. Dissonance between characters often is rooted in struggles characters experience within themselves. A woman's stubborn pride, for example, might contribute to the misery in her marriage, even if her husband does treat her badly. And his behavior towards her might result from his unconscious need to protect himself from being hurt.

Each person is like a fine violin. It doesn't take much to put it out of tune. Consider an orchestra tuning up. What if each instrument is horribly out of tune? Or, perhaps they begin in tune and then something goes horribly awry with the strings and they don't stop to fix it. So it is for drama and human experience. We want the characters in our lives to be in tune, including ourselves, but we find that hard to accomplish. And all it takes is for one person to create havoc for everyone else. This principle of dissonance and tuning applies whether a play is serious or comic. Some plays end with dissonance unresolved; audience recognition is the resolution.

Avoid stereotypes or clichés about behavior based on gender, race, sexual orientation, class and so forth. Each character has a rich inner life and struggles with being "in tune." The black maid in Bruce Norris's *Clybourne Park* tries to control her anger at her white employer's clueless patronizing rather than play the stereotypical role of an obedient two-dimensional servant, contributing tension that is both dramatic and thematic.

WRITING EXERCISES FOR TODAY:

Write about the character that might anchor your action. If you're writing an ensemble piece with several important characters, choose a major figure. If dialogue and monologues come to mind, please write those. If you have time, repeat these exercises with another character.

1. Why do you think this will be an important character? What part will that character play in moving your play forward?
2. What makes that character go "out of tune" and why? How does this manifest itself? Does s/he know this about herself/himself?
3. Will this character change during the course of the play? (Sometimes they don't, like Moliere's Misanthrope.) What actions of others might help that character change or not?
4. What is this character's most important relationship with another character? How does s/he treat that other person? How does the other respond?
5. Do you think this relationship will change over the course of the play? How? Why?

Until tomorrow,

Linda

DAY 6

"[T]o write to your best abilities, construct your own tool box. . . . Then, instead of looking at a hard job and getting discouraged, you will perhaps seize the correct tool and get immediately to work."

—**Stephen King**

YOUR AUDIENCE AND YOUR STAGE

Hi Writers,

When you envision characters and scenes in your mind's eye, you see a stage. Make that as concrete as possible for yourself now. You are writing for what an audience will *see* every bit as much as for what they will *hear*. Today you'll focus on the stage and the play's relationship with your audience. Soon we'll fold theatrical elements such as scenery into daily practice.

Visualize a bare theatrical stage so your characters will be grounded and you'll avoid impractical choices. That doesn't mean the play can only be performed on a stage just like what you imagine but this will make the action more vivid as you write. Be open to letting that stage shape change as you write. Are you imagining a small stage in a small theatre? Or a large one in a large theatre? Does the stage thrust into the audience or is it contained in a proscenium frame? Does the audience surround the action? Do you imagine more than one stage—perhaps a play in which the audience must travel from one place to another? Or, an environmental stage (i.e., a play about a restaurant set in an actual restaurant)? Indoors or outdoors?

Be aware of the relationship your characters/actors might have with your audience, and why. You might start with a conventional fourth wall illusion, but in developing your ideas you could realize something more flexible works better. Consider all the alternatives. When your play is produced the director and design team might develop something different from what you've imagined, just as today plays by Shakespeare and the Greek dramatists are performed in ways quite different from their original productions. Each play begins, though, with a concrete vision.

WRITING EXERCISES FOR TODAY:

1. Describe or sketch the theatre and stage you have in mind for your play and discuss why you are making this choice.
2. Do you imagine using more than one space? Why and how?
3. Will this be an environmental event? Why and how?
4. Do you want a fourth wall illusion or the flexibility to break with that illusion (for example, characters address the audience directly or leave the stage to walk into the audience area)? How might these choices serve your idea?
5. Who do you imagine is your "ideal audience"? Why?
6. Imagine one or more of your characters entering the stage space and walking across it. S/he stops along the way and comments about the space and how s/he feels in it—to her/himself or to the audience or to another character.

Until tomorrow,
Linda

DAY 7

"What I have in mind when I start to write would fit inside an acorn—an acorn, moreover, that rarely if ever grows into an oak. . . . You start with an acorn and you end up with a mackerel. . . . Chance and staying power. That's the hand the imagination's dealt."

—**PHILIP ROTH**

LOOKING BACK AND LOOKING AHEAD

Hi Writers,

Review the lessons for each week and what you've written as you go. Reflect on what you're learning about yourself and writing. The more conscious you are of lessons learned the more they'll become a part of you and help you progress in the weeks—and years—ahead. Don't worry if you don't see the whole picture now for your play. That's normal and healthy.

In the third and fourth weeks of this course, you will devise a *plot* (each incident and revelation of information is a *plot point*) from the broader story and world you have created. You will arrange those plot points into a rough *scenario* before you begin drafting the play. That scenario and those plot points will probably change as you discover the play, but they anchor your work.

Look back and ahead for your characters as well. Unless they die in the course of the play, your characters' lives will continue after this slice of action you're choosing, just as they began before the drama opens. We encounter them in a moment from a larger fabric, like watching a train car pass by a window. The Ladies in *for colored girls who have considered suicide / when the rainbow is enuf* stand for women who will play out stories like theirs unless they heed the play's lessons. The end of a play is not necessarily the end of a character. When Oedipus blinds himself and leaves Thebes, which is where the best-known of Sophocles's plays ends, he goes to his home town of Colonus. Later his daughters, Antigone and Ismene, clash with their dead mother's brother, Creon.

Henrik Ibsen was accused of faulty character work when he had Nora walk out of the door of *A Doll's House* with no way to earn a living or survive as a decent woman in her society. He retaliated by writing *Hedda Gabler*, in which his educated and pregnant title character commits suicide rather than become trapped forever in beige conformity. What other choices are there for "proper women"? he asked, and, perhaps, what are you going to do about it?

WRITING EXERCISES FOR TODAY:

Each character is the main person in his/her life story. Write that story for each character.

1. Write that person's life story as it relates to the world of your play, including what will happen to the character after the drama concludes.
2. Which events and people in that life story have played the greatest role in shaping that character? Why? How?

Until tomorrow,
Linda

---

3 characters: journalist
MARGO - crashed + killed father
① Actress smart, vulnerable, addictive
Chris *② gorgeous - ambitious - liar finance*
Carol *③ housewife - coulda, woulda, shoulda,*
finance - gives up for actor, man.

no-one has children

WEEK 1: THOUGHTS AND REMINDERS

- No one else can write your play.

- You'll discover the play as you write.

- Collect ideas and images, turning them upside down and inside out, exploring without censoring.

- Idea dictates form—you discover the right form. Don't wedge your ideas into a template.

- Write to learn about yourself and your process.

- Practice writing stream-of-consciousness, jotting random thoughts and fragments without editing or second-guessing.

- Your play will be a slice taken from a larger dramatic world and story and from the characters you invent within those.

- You are building dramatic characters, looking for their inner contradictions and dissonance, imagining their flaws and blind spots, exploring the tensions and bonds in their relationships.

- Back up everything you write in a computer and save it elsewhere as well so you can't lose it.

- Use standard script formatting if possible.

- Explore the fictional environments, event(s), place(s), and situation(s) that bring your characters together.

- Describe and/or sketch the stage on which your play will take place.

- Describe how you see your characters' relationships with their audience.

WEEK 2

CREATING CHARACTER DIMENSIONS

This week investigate characters' pasts, create distinctive voices and diction for them, and "show" them with theatrical elements. You will explore possible themes. Using the wealth of material you are gathering, you will begin work on plot in Week 3.

DAY 8

*"What generally inspires me to write is some mysterious
obsession. The nature of the obsession is a little bit like
the obsession one feels sometimes about a dream: You
wake up and feel haunted by persons, presence, a life, an
event or a feeling."*

—MARIA IRENE FORNES

SHOWING THE ACTION

Hi Writers,

Vivid drama often occurs without words. What the Greek philosopher
Aristotle called "spectacle" I call "*theatricality.*" Besides the characters,
scenery, objects, and costumes, theatricality includes lighting and sound,
the theatre space itself and possibly multiple spaces. Silence can be a part
of theatricality, as can physical gestures.

The theatrical items you call for aren't mere set dressing or period
flair—they contribute to theme, character, and story. They enrich the forward movement of a scenario while giving the audience sensory experiences to associate with your main ideas. Theatrical elements add layers
to a drama. They punctuate scenes to help the audience pay attention to
detail or they divert the audience in order to surprise. They provide fun,
generate suspense and evoke awe. They should be appropriate and in pro-
portion to the play's overall design.

Theatrical elements stimulate the audience to join you in "play," to
make connections among objects, sounds, people and story. If I put a rake
onstage, I can't control each audience member's associations with a rake.
However, I can predict that most recognize its common usage and will visualize raking something, perhaps leaves, hay or gravel. Now suppose my

main character's husband just died and she comments that he did all the yard work. The way she looks at the rake, the way she touches it, can imply her feelings for him without a word spoken. That will spark an imaginative and visceral link between the character and the audience.

Curse of the Starving Class opens on a kitchen littered with debris from a broken door. A character brings in a maggot-riddled lamb and the man who broke the door arrives with a bag of artichokes. Without words Sam Shepard's play about Americans who have food but are "starving" from emotional and intellectual malnourishment points to this family's dysfunction.

Suzan-Lori Parks's *Topdog/Underdog* begins with Booth playing 3-card monte. His sleight-of-hand commands audience attention and tells us this man practices deceit. The game symbolizes Booth's brother Lincoln's success as a con man, a life Lincoln is trying to escape. Parks introduces character and theme while foreshadowing the play's tragic crisis and climax.

The first image in *The Dance and the Railroad* by David Henry Hwang is a "Chinaman railroad worker" in the U.S.: "A mountaintop. Afternoon. Lone is practicing Chinese opera steps. He swings his pigtail around like a fan." Hwang merges Chinese tradition with workers imported to build the transcontinental railroad, fixing the play's basic action and metaphors.

Adrienne Kennedy created startling images to signal immediately to audiences that her plays would not unfold realistically. Bright light reveals The Columbia Pictures Lady in the beginning of *A Movie Star Has to Star in Black and White* as she sets the scenes and style of the play in a monologue alternating straightforward narrative with private internal thoughts.

Engage your audience's thoughts, memories and senses without words.

WRITING EXERCISES FOR TODAY:

1. For each character, imagine at least one theatrical element that can convey something important about him or her. Write about its meaning for the character as well as the effect its use might have on your audience. (To help your thinking: Is there an object that appears at some point with which the character has a strong emotional connect? A recurring sound—like a foghorn or a passing train—that stimulates associations and meaning? Something in the clothing, the light, a melody that functions theatrically for your character(s) and us?)

2. Does any element have meaning for one or more other characters? How do these various associations affect the characters?

3. What possible effects might these elements have on the dramatic action?

Until tomorrow,
Linda

HOMEWORK FOR THE WEEK

1. Continue imagining your dramatic world.

2. Continue to collect ideas for the play that come to you as if out of nowhere without forcing them into a structure.

3. Collect ideas for theatrical elements.

4. Write any earlier exercises you haven't attempted.

DAY 9

"When a good idea occurs, it has been prepared by a long time of reflection. You have to be patient. We all have what I call the invisible worker inside ourselves: we don't have to feed him or pay him, and he works even when we are sleeping."

—JEAN-CLAUDE CARRIERE

USING THE PAST

Hi Writers,

Discover your characters' pasts and hear their voices. If your play doesn't adhere to conventional story structure, your characters nevertheless choose what to say or do based in part on past experiences. Drama occurs in the present, onstage, because of personalities, relationships, conflicts, heartbreaks, and passions that happened well before curtain time. No matter the structure or style, investigate characters' pasts before the action you envision. The more you know that past from the inside out, the better you can create the slice of drama onstage.

A wealthy woman's past drives Friedrich Durrenmatt's *The Visit*: Claire offers a fortune to her hometown if residents will kill the man who wronged her there in her youth. The question of what happened to a woman's dead son circles around characters in John Guare's *Language of the Body*, setting up a scenario that weaves in and out of the past. The past could be called the main character in *Old Times*, by Harold Pinter— an investigation of memory, identity and relationships. Even characters in *Waiting for Godot* have pasts; Vladimir claims Godot said before the play begins that he would come, and Pozzo speaks of how Lucky used to behave.

Clybourne Park, by Bruce Norris, opens as a couple prepares to move, having just sold their house. The husband is supposed to bring a trunk down from upstairs, but we don't know its importance. The writer piques curiosity by referring to the past without explanation. Later we learn the couple's Korean War veteran son returned home to neighbors who shunned him because he had killed people. Tormented, he committed suicide upstairs. The trunk is his, from the war. His father plans to bury it as a way of putting the past behind them. When a neighborhood representative tries to persuade the couple not to sell the house to a black family, the homeowner blows up and the play explodes into an indictment against the way society creates and treats "the other." At play's end we see the son in a memory scene and hear the letter he wrote before his suicide. The past has the final word in the present.

WRITING EXERCISES FOR TODAY:

Write these exercises as monologues by the characters so you can hear their voices.

1. Speaking as each character: "One thing about my past that might surprise you is . . . "
2. What from the past makes each character smile?

3. What from the past makes each character unhappy?
4. What do your characters need from one another? (Do they know why? Or might they just think they know why but not know what you as the writer believe is the real reason?)

Until tomorrow,
Linda

DAY 10

"The way people spoke, in short, clipped phrases or long, flowing rambles, revealed so much about them: their place of origin, their social class, their temperament . . . and beneath their temperament, their true nature."

—SALMAN RUSHDIE

CHARACTER VOICE

Hi Writers,

Work today on developing your characters' voices and speaking styles. While they will inevitably have some of your voice in them, they must also be different from you and (usually) from each other. Inventing personalities is one of the most enjoyable aspects of dramatic writing. In writing a play you step aside objectively, and yet you also inhabit the characters' feelings and thoughts. The more you create individuals with their own voices and styles the better you can stand outside them.

To give your characters distinct voices, it may help to imagine each one as someone you know or a performer, public figure, or celebrity who speaks in a way you can easily mimic. Imagine the play cast with actors you think fit the roles. Think of people you've seen in interviews or watched perform whose voices and speaking styles are quickly recognizable. Do any of them "fit" with one of your characters? You won't necessarily copy that public person, but something about his/her style can help you begin to create your character.

Listen for people whose manner of speaking stands out and makes you want to hear what they're saying. It isn't the purpose of theatre to give us what we can hear in ordinary conversation. You're selecting from "real" speech, not merely imitating it. Analyze what makes that speech "special," what makes you want to listen. Observe how short, clipped sentences or a long running hodge-podge of a sentence can distinguish a character. Similarly, dropping the "g" at the end of a word or not can make a difference.

The following examples illustrate tactics writers use to indicate voice and diction.

Lee, in Sam Shepard's *True West*: "So they take off after each other straight into an endless black prairie. The sun is just comin' down and they can feel the night on their backs. What they don't know is that each one of 'em is afraid, see."

Lincoln, in Suzan-Lori Parks' *Topdog/Underdog*: "All around the whole arcade is buzzing and popping. Thuh whirring of thuh duckshoot, baseballs smacking the back wall when someone misses the stack of cans, some woman getting happy cause her fella just won the ring toss. The Boss playing the barker talking up the fake freaks. The smell of the ocean and cotton candy and rat shit."

Howard, in Charles Mee's *The Investigation of Murder in El Salvador*: "I've always worked with decent people, whatever the situation I've been in, however bad things have gotten: you think people were always animals but that's bullshit bullshit because I have never been associated with anyone but people who have read Plato St. Augustine that sort of thing Acquinas even I'm talking about you know what's-his-name Penny knows I'm talking about Averell, I don't care what you might think well, sure, a man with that kind of money, you know, 300, 400 shirts in every closet but that's bullshit bullshit because even Averell comparatively speaking. And he returned my phone calls."

WRITING EXERCISES FOR TODAY:

For each character, try at least one of the following in a monologue:

1. Tell of something in the past that frightened him/her.
2. Express what s/he really thinks but won't say about another character.
3. Describe what a perfect day would be like for him/her.

Until tomorrow,
Linda

DAY 11

"There's an old acting maxim, 'When playing a miser, stress his generosity.'"

—**Alan Ayckbourn**

DUALITIES

Hi Writers,

Imagine inner contradictions and dualities within your characters. It's often said that our strengths are our weaknesses, and vice versa. This was true of Oedipus, for he was a strong and courageous leader who impulsively promised to save his people from plague but was blind to how that very impulsiveness is what led him to kill the stranger in the crossroad—his father. That blindness and that murder were the cause of the plague.

Often a person's first impression masks something very different within. Give your characters opportunities to shed masks and surprise with what they reveal. Although Martha appears to be stronger than her husband George early in *Who's Afraid of Virginia Woolf?*, George takes control of the action and of her by the end, revealing that the nature of their relationship was masked at the beginning. The Greek cultural hero Odysseus is a conniving trickster whose lying ways fail to serve him when he tries to force wounded warrior Philoctetes to carry the bow of Herakles to Troy. Odysseus must tell the truth and face the consequences.

A person might deliberately have two "selves." In Berthold Brecht's *Good Person of Szechuan* a benevolent woman disguises herself as a ruthless capitalist to survive. Young Prince Hal pretends to be a scoundrel so when it's time for him to ascend the throne as Henry V he will seem to have become an entirely new person. He demonstrates that to be powerful a man must know how to play many roles. Blanche in *A Streetcar Named Desire* sings, "But it wouldn't be make believe if you believed in me." Her

Southern belle mask dissolves when she turns in fury on Stanley for ruining her chances with Mitch.

WRITING EXERCISES FOR TODAY:

Write the following exercises in your characters' voices.

1. Explore dualities/contradictions for each character by having one character observe these in another, in monologue.
2. Is there a difference between a character's public presentation and private behavior (if you didn't address that in the exercise above)? If the character is aware of this, have that character speak about it in monologue.
3. Is one of your characters deliberately masking his/her inner nature? How? Why?
4. Will the audience's first impression of one or more of your characters be challenged in the course of the play? How? Why?
5. Imagine something in each major character's inner nature that might emerge as tension mounts and will play a role in generating action, possibly in crisis and climax (if you haven't explored this in the above exercises).

Until tomorrow,
Linda

DAY 12

"I very much write from characters. Those people start speaking, and then I have them in the house with me and I live with them. Then at some point, it's time to get them out of the house. . . . But it is very like having the company of these people and trying to craft them in some way into a story."

—WENDY WASSERSTEIN

ILLUMINATING DIFFERENCES

Hi Writers,

Plays use theatricality to amplify character conflict while also focusing the audience on key aspects of theme and story.

Music: Mark Rothko is painting while listening to "contemplative classical music" as *Red* begins. Just as he controls his studio, Rothko controls the music in it. He plays classical music again in Scene 2. Scene 3 begins with his assistant Ken alone onstage, working with no music playing. With this we glimpse Ken as different from his boss, but not in control. Rothko enters and puts a classical recording on the phonograph. With that he claims authority over his studio. Alone again at the beginning of Scene 4 (the crisis point of a five scene play), Ken is listening to jazz. This is a theatrical confirmation of the change happening in Rothko's studio.

Hearing jazz as he enters, Rothko fumes, "When you pay the rent, you can pick the records." Rothko doesn't recognize or like this music, which demonstrates he is out of synch with the contemporary culture beginning to take over his generation. The scene erupts into arguments—all without music. This palpable quiet suggests they are on a level playing field. Classical music blares as Scene 5 begins with Rothko alone. The aggressive sound signals that while he has regained control he is internally dissonant. In this climactic scene Rothko's bluster fails to hide his uneasy awareness that there is a new breed of artists, and he isn't one of them. Music demonstrates that his mask has slipped.

Object: On a smaller scale, the white woman who is moving from her

Clybourne Park home (Bev) offers a chafing dish she says she never uses to her black maid (Francine). The maid must be polite and subservient in declining it. Bev doesn't give up easily, which makes the exchange even more awkward for Francine. This happens within moments of the beginning of the play. As we watch Bev hold the silver dish between her and Francine, we see clearly the power differential between the two, which Bev doesn't appear to recognize.

Later in the first act, which focuses on race relations, Francine's husband Albert arrives. The black couple is in the middle of a dramatic storm roiling white characters in Bev's living room. Francine, we learn, was the person who found Bev's son upstairs after he'd committed suicide. Now the black couple just wants out of this house. Bev asks Francine if she's taking the chafing dish—no, Francine repeats politely while maintaining her dignity. Then Bev tries to force the chafing dish on Albert—who blows up, "*Ma'am, we don't want your things. Please. We got our own things.*" Note that he calls her "Ma'am," continuing to respect their different social roles even as he struggles to assert himself.

With the chafing dish, playwright Bruce Norris gives us concrete visual images of the place of a black couple in that white world while the white people are arguing over whether or not a black family should be allowed to move into that neighborhood. The exchanges Bev has with Francine and Albert show that while she means to be open and inclusive she has no idea the degree to which she presumes dominance and privilege.

WRITING EXERCISES FOR TODAY:

1. If you have a main character, imagine that character paired off with each of the others. Imagine a theatrical element—visual or aural—that has meaning for the main character that each of the other characters somehow sees differently and can be a source of conflict. (You might not use this item in the play—don't feel restricted.) If there is no main character, write these exercises with the important characters.
2. Write each character's reaction to or feelings about that item in monologue.
3. If dialogue comes easily and character voices are distinctly separate, write character reactions in dialogue.

Until tomorrow,
Linda

DAY 13

"The role of the artist is exactly the same as the role of the lover. If I love you, I have to make you conscious of the things you don't see."

—JAMES BALDWIN

WHAT'S IT ALL ABOUT?

Hi Writers,

A "theme" is the idea the play asks an audience to entertain. Although a play isn't an essay, it should inspire feelings and thoughts. Themes are the "filling" that connects dramatic elements, the "soul" of a play. Some writers begin with a theme in mind while others discover as they write. Playwright Charles Mee reminds us, "[W]riting is not saying something, it is about discovering something." Explore the possible thematic content of your play so you can incorporate it into characters, plot, theatricality and language from the beginning. Think of it as a seed that can open the better you know your play. If it is elusive—you will discover it.

Oedipus and *Topdog/Underdog* demonstrate tragic consequences of being blind to ourselves and lacking control over our desires. Both Sophocles and Suzan-Lori Parks show compassion for their characters, for humankind, rather than wag a lecturing finger. *Boy Gets Girl* leads us to reflect on the ways in which men and women see, hear, and interpret each other. Writer Gilman doesn't preach her themes; she shows situations, conflicts, consequences and coping mechanisms that illustrate them. Each character offers a perspective, and those perspectives change as the drama unfolds. We decide for ourselves what we learn. Comedy asks an audience to laugh at human failings and foolishness. Moliere's *Tartuffe* exposes with humor religious hypocrites who create cult followings for their own gain, for example. The play also shines a spotlight on gullible people who blindly follow Tartuffes.

It is helpful to have more than one theme so each plays off the other(s) and helps the other(s) resonate. In *Boy Gets Girl* the theme of male/female differences intertwines with the action in which Theresa is challenged to be authentic and decisive. In the end she and her male colleagues see each other more as friends and allies than as gender stereotypes.

As you write you will struggle to find ways not to hit the audience over the head with a message but rather let characters argue and examine the views, shadings, confusions, and rationales associated with your theme. A theme is dynamic—not just a slogan that is repeated but rather a philosophical or metaphysical discovery (or set of discoveries) that emerges as characters interact and reveal themselves. It should be challenged, it should expand. If you can't avoid being didactic in this first draft, so be it. You can hone the themes in rewriting.

WRITING EXERCISES FOR TODAY:

1. Write about your feelings, beliefs, questions, and confusions about the theme(s) in your play. Be honest about personal experiences with this theme. Be specific about actions you took or actions taken against or for you.
2. What do you hope to learn by exploring the theme(s) as you write the play?
3. Have your character(s) tell stories about other people that relate to the theme—the people don't have to be in the play. The stories can be memories or hearsay, confessionals or lies. These can be stories to entertain an audience and each other. Or, they can be stories used to threaten or hurt other characters. The stories don't have to wind up in your play either—they are for your process.

Until tomorrow,
Linda

DAY 14

"As a writer, your charge is to create a story that tells all sides and yet illuminates the human condition in such a way that is complex, provocative and fair."

—CHERYL WEST

BEGINNING DIALOGUE

Hi Writers,

Drama happens because characters' backgrounds and personalities propel them forward out of need, fear, blindness, determination, impulse, obligation—many reasons you're beginning to identify. These characters' interactions drive the play and carry themes. In a one-person show characters referred to provide these interactions (just because a character isn't onstage doesn't mean that person isn't contributing to drama).

The language you employ to illuminate interactions and themes helps the audience join in "play." You've been working in monologue with some dialogue. Now that you know your characters better and are beginning to hear their voices, put those characters into dialogue. There is a chicken and egg quality to dramatic writing, an endless loop— you discover their voices in monologue in order to create dialogue with distinctive speakers, yet as characters speak with one another you'll gain a better sense of their voices and personalities.

Who we are with other people can be different from who we are alone with our thoughts. And who a character is with one person can be different from the way s/he is with another. The dramatist explores and reveals this in dialogue.

Each character must speak differently from the others—how much differently depends on the world and relationships you've created. It's challenging not to have all the characters sound like you or change their voices as they interchange thoughts. Characters should be consistent— unless it's in a character's nature to be changeable like a chameleon (and even that requires some consistency).

Don't be frustrated if you have trouble keeping them "in voice." The more your characters speak, the better you'll know those voices.

Writing freely is the ultimate goal for you in this class, not writing perfectly.

WRITING EXERCISES FOR TODAY:

1. Pick up plays you own and read dialogue from them at random. Pay attention to how characters force reactions from each other. Analyze how each one's diction, vocabulary and rhythms are consistent and distinct from the other's mode of expression.
2. Have one character teach another how to do something. The one being taught should either have difficulty understanding or contradict the other or somehow make this an exchange filled with confusion or tension. The outcome can be serious or funny or, what you will. (Try this exercise with several pairings of characters if you have more than two.)
3. Have two characters argue over their memory of a shared experience. (Try this exercise with several pairings of characters if you have more than two.)
4. Have two characters argue over which TV show or movie to watch, or perhaps over what music to listen to, what kind of food to eat. (Try this exercise with several pairings of characters if you have more than two.)
5. When you finish these exercises, read aloud for differences and consistency.

Until tomorrow,
Linda

WEEK 2: THOUGHTS AND REMINDERS

- Investigate how your drama can be shown without words.

- Theatrical elements can amplify characters, actions, and themes.

- A play should inspire feelings and thoughts.

- Two or more themes can help each other resonate.

- Explore dualities and contradictions within characters.

- What happens in your play has been prepared by characters' pasts.

- Each character should have a consistent and distinct "voice" that is different from other characters' voices.

- The "invisible worker" in your subconscious is helping you develop your play. The more you imagine, the more that invisible worker helps you imagine.

- With dialogue, characters force reactions from each other.

<u>WEEK 3</u>

DESIGNING ACTIVE PLOT POINTS

Y ou will identify and list the events and information that should be enacted or communicated in your play—without concern for how you will arrange them. You will add complexity to your main characters while considering how secondary characters relate to the main characters and contribute to the drama.

DAY 15

"A strong enough situation renders the whole question of plot moot, which is fine with me. The most interesting situations can usually be expressed as a 'what if' question: What if vampires invaded a small New England village?"

—**STEPHEN KING**

FROM CHARACTER AND DRAMATIC WORLD TO PLOT

Hi Writers,

Today take the first steps towards defining key incidents that dramatize your idea, your "What if(s)?" Select those incidents from your larger story and dramatic world. Each incident is a *plot point*; all of them constitute your plot. Spin as many plot points as you can for this world you're imagining. Don't rush into deciding how to arrange them (that's the scenario, which we'll address beginning Day 22).

Some plot points set up the "what if?" that engages the audience in the Beginning. Other plot points follow as consequences and further stimuli. That's where the substance of the action develops. You now have the luxury and challenge of playing with the potential of your idea, ruling out clichés, discovering which consequences excite you the most. As you write the first draft you will discover the plot more fully and be open to making changes. You start, though, with ideas about where you want to go on your journey.

Think of plot points both as *events* and as *information*. Events and the dispensation of information might happen on or offstage. You don't have to decide now where or how this will happen. "Events" are actions characters take alone as well as exchanges between and among characters—those can be confrontational, playful, confessional, deceitful, and so forth. There is an active exchange, a cause and effect, pushing and pulling, or perhaps a transformation in the relationship(s). Usually these are verbal, but it is possible to have a very powerful nonverbal event such as "love at first sight."

"Information" is facts we need to know about these people and/or about the dramatic world and story. Information can refer to a past event, like a divorce, that will play an important role in the action. It can include a character's habit of treating people. If we learn a character is typically brusque or evasive, that behavior can be significant but it isn't dramatic in and of itself. You can ease yourself into drafting the play if you leave for later the question of how you will handle each piece of information. First—identify the information that is necessary for characters and/or the audience.

Approach your work on plot by focusing on your main character. This person, called the protagonist in literary theory, centers the situation and the drama. S/he might drive it through an overt desire, or be driven by other characters. Begin your plot work with the one whose choices and changes probably will go the greatest distance and carry the most weight dramatically. Antigone's determination to give her brothers a proper burial, against her Uncle Creon's wishes, forces all the events in Sophocles's play by her name. The title character in Horton Foote's *Vernon Early* says little and has almost no confrontations while he tends to everyone as a small town doctor. He centers the play without being the agent behind the play's events. We learn about him from others' gossip, so that by the end we are moved to tears by grief he experiences but does not share with those around him.

If your characters are an ensemble and no one is the protagonist, work today with any of them who are particularly crucial to the play's forward movement. For example, in Euripides' *The Trojan Women* all the characters react to their fates at the end of the Trojan War but Queen Hecuba possibly suffers most.

Events involving your main character will be major plot points in your drama—not the only ones and not the only important ones. They will form the *spine* of the structure. That main character's needs, wants, personality, past, habits, fears and beliefs will all come into play in determining what will happen dramatically. It isn't dramatic for a character to merely "want" something—rather, ask what a character does to put that "want" into action. Drama occurs when what one character wants clashes or meshes with what another wants, when characters throw one another into dissonance and struggle to right themselves. Consider what the *stakes* are for your characters with each plot point. The stakes should be as high, as intense, as meaningful as possible. If something goes wrong for your characters, what will that mean for them? What's the worst that can happen and how can you bring an audience into the suspense that might generate?

WRITING EXERCISES FOR TODAY:

1. Experiment with phrasing your dramatic idea as a "What if?" situation.
2. Write in two lists all the plot points you can imagine for your main character. Call the first list "Yes" and the second "Maybe." That will help you sort out which you feel at this point you want to include in the play from those you might or might not include (list plot points whether onstage or not, whether events or information). If all are on the "Maybe" list, that's fine. By keeping your focus on the main character now, you can establish key plot points.

    Don't try to organize them in the order in which they'll be staged or told. If they fall into a certain order, let that happen, but keep in mind that you might change that order. When you don't fret over whether or not you want an idea and when you don't concern yourself with the order of events, you should feel free to write down everything you can imagine that will occur with your main character.

    Include information that must be revealed about that character, theatrical elements that will be used, stories the character will tell, stories others will tell about that character, clashes and confidences with other characters, physical gestures by that character. Whether you imagine five or fifty plot points isn't important now.
3. Write as much as you can about each event—why it's happening, what it will mean to the characters, to the action and theme, to the audience.
4. As you look over those plot points, indicate with an asterisk or another method those that might simply be information rather than active events.

5. Review the plot points in the "Yes" list and ask what the stakes are for your main character in each event. Can the stakes be higher within the play's logic and style? If so, consider how to raise the stakes.

Until tomorrow,
Linda

HOMEWORK FOR THE WEEK

1. Continue developing lists of possible plot points you begin on Days 15 and 16.

2. Continue imagining active ways to illustrate your characters' complexities, using exercises in the back of the book if necessary.

3. Continue exploring how to show the action and theme theatrically, using exercises in the back of the book if necessary.

DAY 16

"Real things are the starter dough by which the baker bakes the bread."

—ALICE MUNRO

REAL CHARACTERS / REAL PLOTS

Hi Writers,

Your characters' behavior, feelings and memories are the "real things" Alice Munro refers to. Delve into your own deeply felt personal experiences. Be "in" the feeling when you were betrayed, learned a loved one had died, first felt deep romantic attraction, laughed so hard you could barely breathe. With these visceral memories you excavate character. Characters are always "doing" something onstage, beat by beat. A character *speaks* to accomplish something, whether it is to misdirect, persuade, hurt, the list goes on. And a character *listens* with intention as well—to learn, to plan a rebuttal, to understand, to buy time.

You are practicing inhabiting that character while at the same time stepping outside him/her to place him/her in action with others. It can be useful to interplay a day of working on plot with a day of working on character. Each feeds the other. Characters shouldn't be manipulated to fit into events and events should flow naturally from characters' behavior. Pearl Cleage had to keep it "real" while writing *Blues for an Alabama Sky*: "When I got to the end of this play, I realized I was trying to make Angel do something that had not been justified by the characters and by their story. . . . So I had to come to terms with what it meant for me to create a character who doesn't triumph."

Working on plot points can help you identify questions to ask of your main character. That character's behavior must be plausible and consistent, "real" in terms of something an audience will believe that character would "really" do in each situation. Each play has its own "reality," regardless of style. If your play is more surreal or absurd than conventional "realism," or if it's a collage of images and events, you still have an obligation to give your audience behavior grounded in reality they can grasp. Winnie in Samuel Beckett's *Happy Days* is not going to suddenly give us a reasoned soliloquy on Wittgenstein. Ubu Roi doesn't behave like Henry V because the writer decides to change the character midstream. In Eugene Ionesco's *The Bald Soprano* humor arises from characters who appear like everyday couples chatting in a living room but whose chitchat is banal and inane to a hilarious and yet recognizable extreme. Anchor your audience with something "real."

WRITING EXERCISES FOR TODAY:

Write in your main character's voice. If your cast is an ensemble, choose a significant character.

1. What are your character's sweetest memories?
2. What are vulnerabilities others might not know about? Does the character know of them? Does s/he deliberately hide them? Why?
3. What does your character take pride in? Is this pride misplaced or is it earned? Does the character carry the pride too far?

4. How does your character behave when s/he feels cornered, confused? How does s/he feel when s/he behaves like that?
5. What roles do family and friends outside your drama play in that character's life?

Until tomorrow,
Linda

DAY 17

"Our characters are defined by the actions they take, and their actions are informed by their attempts to get what they want."

—ALAN WATT

SUPPORTING ROLES

Hi Writers,

Today enjoy thinking of characters that don't carry or center the main action in soliloquy, in pairings, or in other groupings. Are these people in conflict, conspiring, confessing? Plot points for these characters should be as specific and active as possible. For example, "Francine struggles to remain civil while Jim and Karl try to force her to agree that black people wouldn't fit into a white neighborhood." They can be as brief as "the Doctor tells Elena he loves her."

A minor plot point can illustrate a supporting character's place in a drama. For example, Rothko's assistant Ken isn't alone on stage until the beginning of Scene 3 in *Red*. A painting wrapped in brown paper is tucked "unobtrusively" in a corner. Ken tells someone on the phone, "I'll show it to him if the moment's right." Throughout the scene we watch for Ken to show his painting to Rothko; he doesn't. What if that event had been occurred at the play's beginning, before we know either man? Or later, when Ken asserts himself? By placing the wrapped painting in the middle of the scenario, the writer gives us time to understand why Ken would hesitate and also generates curiosity as we wonder how Rothko might respond.

Ma Rainey insists that her stuttering nephew record the introduction to her signature song and be paid for it. That insistence introduces humor and pathos to the play as we wait with all the characters for the young man, a minor character, to get through it correctly. The episode demonstrates Ma's control over others as well as her soft side. Minor characters can have their own moments in the sun while they enhance the main spine of the play.

WRITING EXERCISES FOR TODAY:

1. Write in two lists all the plot points you can imagine for your supporting characters. Create a separate list for each character. If you only have time for one character today, select the one that might have the most powerful effect on the main character. As you did for the protagonist, call the first list "Yes" and the second "Maybe." Include information that must be revealed about that character, theatrical elements that will be used, stories the character will tell, stories others will tell about that character, clashes and confidences with other characters, physical gestures by that character. Don't try to organize them in the order in which they'll be staged or told. The quantity of plot points isn't important.

2. Write as much as you can about each event—why it's happening, what it will mean to the characters and to the audience.

3. As you look over those plot points, indicate with an asterisk or another method those that might simply be information that needs to be revealed rather than active events.

Until tomorrow,
Linda

DAY 18

> *"The meeting of two personalities is like the contact of two chemical substances: if there is any reaction, both are transformed."*
>
> —CARL GUSTAV JUNG

CONSIDER CASSANDRA

Hi Writers,

Actors often remind themselves that there are no small roles. Each character contributes to the overall fabric of the play, whether it is to the action or theme or in some other way. The stronger the minor characters, the more they inspire you to strengthen your main character. So, consider Cassandra, a minor character in the first complete Greek drama we have from the 5th century BC, Aeschylus's *Agamemnon*. The title character brings Trojan princess Cassandra home to Mycenae with him as his slave mistress. She waits, saying nothing, while his wife Clytemnestra confronts him outside the palace and forces Agamemnon to walk the blood-red royal carpet to his death inside. Next Clytemnestra tries to persuade Cassandra to follow. Unmoving and silent, Cassandra's presence alone is a vivid reminder of the horrors of the Trojan War.

Only when Clytemnestra exits into the palace does Cassandra speak. She describes the assassination happening inside and conjures the chaotic passions overtaking Mycenae before going inside to her own certain death. Her wild prophetic song and dialogue with the Choral Leader is one of the most extraordinary scenes in all of dramatic literature. The main action of that play can happen without Cassandra, but it would lose dynamism and texture. Cassandra provides a counterpoint to the main characters that amplifies theme and tragedy.

Zillah in Tony Kushner's *A Bright Room Called Day* is another example of counterpoint. The main drama takes place in 1930s Germany. All the characters except Agnes try first to resist and then to escape the oncoming Nazi horror. Agnes is a protagonist who does not change, who will not leave her room. Zillah is a woman in the 1980s; for her the social catastrophe is the early pandemic of AIDS. She sits reading while behind her on a screen is an image of a Hitler rally in which all but one woman raise their arms in the Nazi salute. Kushner interrupts the story of Agnes intermittently with interludes of Zillah and that image, which zooms closer and closer to the dissenting woman each time we see it. The climax of the play merges Zillah, the image and Agnes' room together with music and other elements that carry the totality of the play beyond Agnes' story. That merger foregrounds the need to act, to resist dehumanization and genocide.

WRITING EXERCISES FOR TODAY:

Explore plot points you've identified and imagine more.

1. What's happening in that confrontation between X and Y that can carry one or more of your themes?
2. What might have led to that confrontation?
3. What might it spark for further action?
4. How are the characters feeling about this event?
5. What in this event can be surprising and enjoyable for the audience?
6. How is the broader "frame" or context of your dramatic world affecting characters' actions and relationships?
7. Do any of your characters serve as counterpoint, like Cassandra or Zillah, more than actually driving the play forward? How? Why?
8. Enjoy spinning further ideas about minor characters—what in their personalities might lend entertainment and texture to your play?

Until tomorrow,
Linda

DAY 19

"Every character should want something, even if it is only a glass of water."

—KURT VONNEGUT

ANTAGONISTS AND ALLIES

Hi Writers,

Consider whether supporting characters are antagonists or confidants/ allies, or perhaps more than one of these. The main character is the "first actor," protagonist, the one Greek dramatists gave the most lines. In time the Greeks added two more actors—the antagonist (second actor) and the tritagonist (third actor). Those three actors played all the roles. Typically the antagonist and tritagonist supplied information and obstacles that forced the protagonist to confront the main issue of the play with responses leading to a conclusion that might or might not involve recognition and personal change. Over time we have become accustomed to giving the title "antagonist" to the character or characters who thwart the main character or force change.

An *antagonist* forges ahead with his/her own life, pursuing desires that cause friction when they encounter or actually collide with the protagonist's. This doesn't always happen out of bad motives. As you think of your characters keep in mind this potential for friction, for sparks that move the drama forward, more than "good" and "bad" characters. For example, the messengers who bring information to Oedipus have no evil intentions, yet what they report leads to his tragic end by making him self-aware. Other antagonists are more obviously in conflict with the main character. Tony stalks Theresa and escalates conflict to the point of putting her life in danger in *Boy Gets Girl*. Sam Shepard's *The Tooth of Crime* pits two characters against one another in classic protagonist/antagonist style as established rock and roll icon Hoss fights newcomer Crow with words and music.

A *confidant* is someone who listens to the main character, sympathizes and might try to help. Think of Juliet's Nurse, of Blanche's sister Stella.

Theresa's male co-workers in *Boy Gets Girl* are confidants, then allies, and finally characters who go through their own self-recognitions and changes because they allied with her. The Policewoman in that play also serves as an ally who remains objective and gives Theresa the facts she needs but at first won't heed.

Imagine someone serving as a confidant and then turning into an antagonist. Iago, for instance, turns on Othello. Peter enters Agnes's motel room in Tracy Letts's *Bug* as a vulnerable ally; his psychosis overwhelms her and pulls her into his insanity. Or, from antatonist to ally: In Sophocles's *Philoctetes,* Odysseus sends Neoptolemus to the island where Philoctetes lives in exile with the goal of persuading the wounded warrior to rejoin the Greek army. However, when Neoptolemus realizes Odysseus tricked him into doing something unethical, he becomes an ally of the exile and an antagonist to Odysseus.

In some plays we might say two main characters serve as twins or *doppelgangers* of each other. For example, study the relationships of brothers in *Topdog/Underdog* and *True West.* One interpretation of Harold Pinter's mysterious *Old Times* is that the character Anna who visits Deely and Kate is a memory of Kate as she once was.

In aristocratic societies, characters were assigned according to their class relationships. Upper-class characters (royalty and the wealth) were coupled romantically or paired in friendships or antagonism, while their servants were similarly paired. A servant could be a confidant to a lord or lady. These characters can further be distinguished by "*type*": wily servant, bombastic pedant, innocent heroine, wise serving-woman, miser, brute, braggart soldier, penny-pinching merchant, and so on. Shakespeare added dimension to some of these "types," creating memorable characters such as Juliet's Nurse or servant Grumio in *The Comedy of Errors.*

WRITING EXERCISES FOR TODAY:

1. Identify each supporting character in relation to the protagonist and action as antagonist or confidant/ally. Write about how each fits one or more supporting role category, what affect that has on the protagonist and themselves, as well as on other characters, action, theme, and aesthetic impact.

2. If one changes from ally to antagonist or vice versa, why and how might that happen?

3. Are they aware they are playing these roles? If so, how might that affect their behavior?
4. Are any of your characters similar to traditional "types"? If so, how might that serve you? If not, does thinking of them as types help you clarify their personalities?

Until tomorrow,
Linda

DAY 20

"I believe all plays are mystery plays."

—JEFFREY HATCHER

BEGIN AT THE END

Hi Writers,

Each play unfolds like a mystery, for even if the audience knows the resolution they don't know how you're going to achieve it or how the production will enact it. The typical mystery/crime structure calls for several possible culprits and several possible resolutions. The closer we get to the ending the fewer options there are for the conclusion. Sometimes even in the final moments, when we think we know who is guilty and how this story will resolve, there's a surprising and yet plausible twist. While building a scenario, you'll make choices to tease the audience and bring them into "play." Writer/director John Donahue told the Minneapolis Children's Theatre Company to act as if you have a lizard in your pocket. As the play proceeds the lizard pokes a bit of itself out of the pocket, a tail here, an elbow there, enough to make the audience want to know more. The actor knows the lizard is there from the beginning.

An old maxim is that the end of a play is foreshadowed in the beginning. Whether or not you think you know the end of your play, devise two or three plausible endings. Giving thought to the ending first will help you identify plot logic you need to get to the conclusion and create more intriguing twists. As you write in the coming weeks your play might blossom into something you didn't anticipate and it might insist on a conclusion you haven't yet imagined. That's all well and good. If it surprises you, it will surprise your audience.

If you're adapting from a familiar story, everyone expects the familiar ending. The focus is on how you get to the end and/or how you'll handle it. That is, how will characters, language, and theatricality interplay in your adaptation to make this known story fresh and unpredictable? You invest "poetic license." Charles Mee uses ancient Greek plays as "scaffolding." The audience focuses on the how and why of his arrangements and language for suspense and surprises. David Henry Hwang based *M. Butterfly* on a news article about a diplomat who fell in love with a Chinese Opera "actress"—by tradition a man—who tricked the diplomat into thinking "he" was female. Hwang added complexity by setting the play in French Colonial Vietnam, turning the actress into a Communist spy, and using echoes of Puccini's opera, *Madame Butterfly*. This added options for the crisis, climax and conclusion.

WRITING EXERCISES FOR TODAY:

1. Devise two or more possible endings for your play. Write them out as thoroughly as possible in terms of which character makes what kind of decision and why, how that affects other characters, how that carries the theme, and what impact it might have on the audience.
2. Does imagining two or more possible endings affect the plot points you've identified so far? Review those to see how you can keep the ending ambiguous as far as possible into the play.

Until tomorrow,
Linda

DAY 21

*"ROTHKO: Most of painting is thinking. . . . Ten percent
is putting paint onto the canvas. The rest is waiting."*
—**JOHN LOGAN,** *Red*

TAKE A GOOD LOOK

Hi Writers,

Before constructing and composing a scenario, review and organize all
that you've done these past three weeks. An artist will often step back to
look at a painting in progress. This is part of the process, not an interruption in your writing. You have volumes of notes on characters, story, plot,
theme, and theatricality. You wrote monologues and dialogues. You made
lists of plot points with commentary. You might have sketched scenes. Review letters and exercises. Try exercises you didn't have time for to help
clarify as needed or spark a fresh idea.

As you review this array of material, you can appreciate the need for
an organized filing system that makes it easy for you to retrieve notes. This
could be in your computer or in "old-fashioned" cardboard files. Everyone
thinks differently, so you must create a system that works for you. You can
organize by categories like plot and theme. You might have files for each
character. Perhaps you have a file for monologues and another for dialogue. As you build the scenario you'll probably file together everything
you think might go into the Beginning section or other sections of the
scenario. However you choose to do this, take time to order the material.

A reminder: Back up everything in your computer or on a flash drive
and/or email files to yourself so you can retrieve them from another computer if needed.

Action statement/logline: Today's lesson asks you to define the action
of your play in no more than two sentences. One would be best. This exercise forces you to pin down the core of the play without mentioning every
character or getting caught up in plot turns. With this you emphasize the
thematic and active fulcrum of your play, what changes, what is learned,
to give you direction for the scenario and writing. Your definition might

change as you write; most likely, it will become clearer to you. People who read for agents and producers give each manuscript a "*logline*," a one sentence description of the core action. Create your own logline.

Following are examples of action statements/loglines. Note that I don't mention the names of characters. These are distillations of action and theme:

- Cinderella — An orphan liberates herself by visualizing and then claiming her best self, with the aid of allies and magic. (The action is liberation, not being found by a prince.) Notice how this differs from a summary of plot points: "This is a story about a young girl whose parents died and who now lives with an evil stepmother. She dreams of … etc."
- *Red* — A celebrated painter challenged by his assistant reclaims artistic integrity while glimpsing he is being eclipsed by a new generation.
- *Boy Gets Girl* — A writer pursued by a potentially violent stalker learns to share with others, be true to herself, and begin a new and more authentic life.

If the action of your play is unclear—that's alright. It will emerge as you write and it might not become clear until the end of the first draft. However, as you begin you have something in mind, a dramatic goal. It's good to find out for yourself if it's clear or not, and if it isn't try to understand what aspect of it remains opaque. Don't be harsh with yourself—simply observe what you do or do not understand at this stage in your journey.

WRITING EXERCISES FOR TODAY:

1. Write questions you still have about characters, story, plot points, etc.
2. What is the context or larger "frame" for your plot ideas? Are you staging a story that requires characters to make decisions? Is it urgent that the play's major drama be enacted in a defined period of time? Are characters gathered for an event that will force to them face challenges and consequences?
3. Which plot points might make an audience wonder, "What happens next?"
4. Describe your action in no more than two sentences, preferably one.

Jot down key words under action and theme; unite them with the journey your main character or ensemble takes. You can begin with several sentences and practice compressing them. You might construct several "loglines" if you aren't sure of the exact action.

5. Write your action statement on a card or slip of paper you keep in sight. It's your North Star.

Until tomorrow,
Linda

WEEK 3: THOUGHTS AND REMINDERS

- The accumulation of events and information that carry and drive a drama is the plot.

- Each event or bit of information needed for your play is a plot point.

- Dramatic events are active—they can be playful, confessional, confrontational or persuasive, among many other possibilities.

- The main character (protagonist) centers the situation and drama. His/her choices and change (or lack of change) are the ones most crucial to the play. It is possible for an ensemble of characters to share that anchoring role.

- Characters' behavior and speech must be plausible and consistent within the dramatic world you're creating.

- Plot ideas lead to asking better questions of characters—character ideas lead to asking better questions of plot.

- Supporting characters play roles with one another and the main character as antagonists, confidants/allies or counterpoints. Sometimes they serve in more than one of these roles.

- A character that isn't critical to the main action can function as counterpoint to heighten the play's themes and aesthetic impact.

- Before you create a scenario and begin a draft, determine as much as possible how characters relate to one another.

- Begin at the end: Design several possible endings so the audience can't predict outcome and you give yourself room for discovery.

- Define the context or larger "frame" for your plot ideas and challenges to characters.

- Describe your play's action in an action statement/logline of no more than two sentences, preferably one.

- Express the situation of your play as "What if X happens," the way Stephen King suggests.

WEEK 4

ARRANGING PLOT POINTS INTO SCENARIO

To prepare to begin your draft in the next unit, you will experiment this week with arranging the plot points into a loose scenario, focusing on the Beginning section. You will decide how to bring an audience into the rules of the game you are creating for them and consider how to lead them through action with beats.

DAY 22

"Everyone I know flails around, kvetching and growing
despondent, on the way to finding a plot and structure
that work. You are welcome to join the club."

—ANNE LAMOTT

BEGINNING THE SCENARIO

Hi Writers,

This week you will outline a scenario—an arrangement of plot points—for
your first draft. You have created a main character (or the primary characters if you're writing for an ensemble). You have in mind an action state-
ment/logline and one or more themes. You have identified some events
that probably will occur in the play as well as information characters and
audience should know. It's quite likely that more plot points will come to
you this week as you write. You have devised two or more possible endings.

Now you make preliminary decisions about the form your idea suggests. Does it want to flow without interruption by an intermission? Do
changes of place suggest clear breaks or continuity? Is the action anchored
by a main character or shared by an ensemble? Will the action loop back
in time or drive forward in a linear manner? Your characters might take
directions you hadn't imagined and the initial plan will change so you can
pursue what is happening organically. While finding the best structure for
your play is challenging, breaking down the process into steps and principles will help. The scenario you create now is not written in stone.

Every play has a Beginning, Middle, and End, whether it runs for ten
minutes or three hours, and proceeds realistically or is a composition of
monologues without a conventional storyline. I'm not calling these "acts"
because one-acts and five-acts and plays that are a series of scenes all have

these three sections. Keep it simple—Beginning, Middle, and End. Usually the Beginning and Ending portions of a play are slightly shorter than the Middle. That might mean one-fourth of the play for the Beginning and Ending, half for the Middle. It's possible to have each section be one-third of the play.

Set up the action, characters, style and intrigue of the play quickly in the Beginning. In the days ahead we'll break that down further into "point of attack," "focus," "inciting incident" and "dramatic intrusions," as well as other terms that might be helpful. Having taken the audience's interest in the Beginning, you play with it through the Middle as you have characters and their dilemmas blossom through conflicts and revelations. Once the complications of the action reach a head (crisis), you'll take the audience into the End through a climax and then contraction or abrupt movement into conclusion.

Here is a simple overview of the way most plays are constructed:
- Grab the audience's attention in the Beginning as you set up style, characters and other "rules of the game."
- Sustain attention with changes and teases that hold back key information while propelling events forward.
- Make the audience wonder, "What's next?"
- Build and modulate intensity to reach the highest peak.
- Save the best for last.

WRITING EXERCISES FOR TODAY:

1. Write each of the plot points for your main character on a note card or slip of paper. Those plot points will be the spine or throughline of your play.
2. Divide the plot points into three groups, depending on where you think they might belong—Beginning, Middle, and End. If you can't decide where a plot point belongs, write it on multiple cards and put one in each group.
3. Spread the plot points for the Beginning out on a table or large surface. Try different arrangements of them until you see one that, for the time being, looks like a good order of events for the Beginning of the play.
4. Do the same for the Middle and End.
5. Read through in sequence the plot points you now have. You should see

the spine of the action emerging with an initial sense of what should happen in which section of the play.

6. Write the sequence you've assembled for each group.

7. If you see several possible arrangements, write out each one.

8. Follow the directions above for sorting out plot points and other ideas you already have into Beginning, Middle, and End.

Until tomorrow,
Linda

HOMEWORK FOR THE WEEK

1. Continue to develop ideas for plot points and possible scenario arrangements until you find a pattern that satisfies you for now. That will be the form you have in mind as you begin writing next week.

2. Continue to collect ideas for your story, plot, characters, logic, relationships, themes, and theatricality. It's possible that in doing that you will discover new ideas and/or changes for the scenario.

3. Work on character exercises in past letters you haven't attempted.

DAY 23

"Start as close to the end as possible."

—**KURT VONNEGUT**

SETTING UP THE GAME

Hi Writers,

Whether you're writing a play that unfolds in a linear and fairly realistic manner or creating a collage of monologues and media images, the Beginning invites the audience into a game that you and they will play for the duration of the performance. The first minutes of a long play (typically called a *"full-length"*) establish some of the "rules" your play will follow about style, setting, characters, theatricality, and language. The audience is working with you, adjusting to these elements. You tease them with just enough about the story about to unfold (or themes, if this is not a conventional story) that they'll "tune in" for more.

The first entry into the world of your play is the *"point of attack."* In a story-based play, it's close enough to the events that will collide into crisis where you can generate and sustain a drama without losing audience attention. As Vonnegut advises, don't ask your audience to meander through episodes that lack tension. *Hamlet* doesn't open with the boy Hamlet and his parents in happy days. The play begins right before Hamlet arrives home after his father's suspicious death. First we see a graveyard, with guards literally spooked by the Ghost of Hamlet's father. This sets up suspense, the presence of death and supernatural foreboding.

If your play doesn't adhere to a conventional storyline with a protagonist, like Thornton Wilder's *Our Town*, you still face the question, "How do I begin?" Your "point of attack" will be an introduction to the themes and theatricality you plan for the play. Wilder constructs his scenario in three acts—in the first he positions the main characters in Grover's Corners, N.H., introducing us to the small town in ordinary moments while at the same time situating characters in his larger theme of human history as we experience them in small ways and in "the Mind of God." The second act focus is a wedding and the third is set in a cemetery. With these events Wilder takes us from young love to death and beyond.

After the point of attack, you launch the action. Something happens that sets in motion events that will cascade through to the end of your play. We call that the "*inciting incident.*" It can take many forms, from an actual physical assault to a simple declaration from one character to another. Because it happens, because it's said, actions and reactions will accelerate until you conclude the game. After the graveyard scene, Hamlet returns home. His tense initial encounter with his mother and Claudius sets up the main character's grief and anger. With Hamlet we hear of the Ghost and go directly into the graveyard. There when the Ghost accuses Claudius of murder, Hamlet becomes obsessed with the quest for truth and revenge. Once the Ghost plants the seed in Hamlet (the inciting incident), the drama moves forward. Shakespeare quickly sets a mood, hooks an audience, introduces the main characters and information briefly, and then sends the main character into dramatic challenges.

When the inciting incident happens is your choice. An audience usually becomes restless after three to five minutes in a short play, or eight to ten minutes in a full-length if they don't have a sense for where this game is going. After fifteen minutes they can begin to drop out if you don't give them direction for the drama ahead. The opening of *Hamlet* doesn't introduce all the characters or all the problems they'll confront. Shakespeare gives only the essential information needed to set the play in motion.

Our Town doesn't have a conventional inciting incident. However, Wilder guides us through his thematic mosaic with his narrator—a Stage Manager who speaks directly to the audience. That character explains in the Beginning he means for this play to tell people a thousand years from now that "this is the way we were—in our growing up and in our marrying, and in our living, and in our dying." In Act I we meet George and Emily as flirting teens, a simple action that sets us up for their courtship and marriage. The ordinary and sweet nature of their relationship makes the final act after Emily's death poignant. Through that couple the Stage Manager brings Wilder's audience into reflections on mortality, which is the play's larger goal.

A play might introduce something in the beginning that seems as if it will be the main focus of the drama but isn't. This "MacGuffin," popularized by filmmaker Alfred Hitchcock, grabs audience attention and brings them into the game while the dramatist takes more time developing the real locus of the play. In *Uncle Vanya*, for example, Chekhov throws us into a crowded rural household whose residents are getting on each other's nerves. This point of attack gives the audience a dissonant dramatic world. But where is the action? Vanya declares his love for Elena early on. That might be the inciting incident, that might be the event that drives the drama, we think. However, as the play unfolds into the Middle and the End, the drama goes in directions we hadn't seen in the Beginning, directions that aren't propelled by Vanya's love for Elena. The story opens into many complications and broken hearts, severed relationships and painfully restricted lives. Chekhov catches the audience's interest with Vanya's protestations of love for Elena to gain time for something richer and unexpected.

If you plan to use techniques other than an unfolding action that maintains the illusion of a "fourth wall" between characters/actors and the audience (such as a narrator and/or framing devices), introduce them from the start. A *narrator* should not take the place of action that can be shown in an entertaining manner that propels the play forward or merely substitute for dialogue. *Our Town's* Stage Manager narrates while also serving as a character, a poetic philosopher who stimulates audience imagination and helps us place ordinary events into cosmic context. Neil Simon's narrator in *Brighton Beach Memoirs* steps in and out of the action as a character to comment on his feelings and other characters in a way that is as entertaining as the episodes.

Some writers use "framing devices" or "bookends" to provide prologue and epilogue to a play. Often a narrator speaks directly to the audience at the beginning to introduce something about the action about to take place and then returns in the end to offer words of conclusion. Shakespeare frames *A Midsummer Night's Dream* with a royal wedding.

For your Beginning, create an active world with intriguing characters and a problem or conflict that will bring an audience into that world. Set up the theatrical style you'll use so the audience can adjust to the rules of your game. Include only the information that absolutely must be conveyed and can be shown in an engaging way. The Beginning says, "Welcome aboard, there's more to come."

WRITING EXERCISES FOR TODAY:

1. Arrange plot points involving supporting characters that might not include your main character into Beginning, Middle, and End categories.
2. Note how these choices help construct the action.
3. As you approach writing the Beginning of your play, identify your point of attack and inciting incident. Be clear with yourself about why you are selecting these and why you think, for now at least, that these are the best choices for you and your audience.
4. Do you have a MacGuffin for your play? If so, what is it and how does it function? If not, think about it. If you choose not to have one, be very clear about why not.
5. If you want to use a narrator or framing devices, be as honest and clear as possible with yourself about why those choices enhance the audience's dramatic experience.

Until tomorrow,
Linda

DAY 24

"All any writer wants is to connect with an audience."
—J. HOLTHAM

RELATING TO YOUR AUDIENCE

Hi Writers,

Whatever its form, your drama should seem logical, with characters who behave consistently. You want the audience with you all the way, saying "Yes I buy that." To accomplish that you must consider objectively the mechanics of dramatic construction.

Probe your play's relationship to your audience. Will your performers at any time turn to address the audience but remain in character? Will an actor break character to speak to the audience and then go back into character? Will more than one character break that fourth wall illusion? Will any characters speak to themselves in soliloquy, not acknowledging the audience but sharing their innermost thoughts? Will some or all of the actors play more than one role? Will you have several characters function as a chorus to comment on and add thematic dimension to the main action? Chekhov's characters at times blur the boundary between illusion and direct address. They spill out their inner thoughts and woes as if talking to themselves while in dialogue with other people. The audience is prepared from first meeting a character to have that person reveal him/herself with little censoring as the play unfolds. You might experiment with that, asking yourself which characters push boundaries and which ones are very protective of what they let others know about themselves.

Your play can go to extremes if you've set up plausibility from the start. Early in *A Movie Star Has to Star in Black and White* Adrienne Kennedy calls for actors made up to look like screen stars Bette Davis and Paul Henreid, which signals an unusual theatrical plan. Caryl Churchill's *Cloud 9* begins with a Victorian family singing a patriotic song, followed by patriarch Clive's rhyming introduction to his wife Betty, who is played by a man; after that an audience should not expect realism. In days ahead I will address flashbacks and "time-bending," if you're considering playing with episodes out of time sequence.

Lynn Nottage's *Mud, River, Stone* uses direct address by narrators, framing, and fourth wall realism. The play begins with direct address by an African-American couple. Sarah and David, who holds a stone, narrate going to Africa "to see the mud and stone ruins of our ancestors." They change into safari gear while describing the journey, telling the audience that their rental car ran out of gas in the rain and the road became a river. The couple walked to a colonial-era hotel. At this point, other characters appear and the play shifts into a play of ideas using fourth wall realism and dialogue in that hotel setting. After grueling ordeals and the dissolution of the couple's naïve romanticism about Africa, "[l]ights begin to fade around all but Sarah and David" while the sound of rain continues. We return to the opening image and direct narrative address.

> SARAH. It rained for another week and then it stopped.
> DAVID. Yes this is the stone.
> SARAH. A reminder. (The rain stops.)

Are you considering using *mediated images* (projections or video, for example)? People usually give more attention to what they see than to what they hear. Projected images can overwhelm speech, so avoid placing important ideas, information, or dramatic revelations in competition with them. Think of mediated images or episodes as plot points and/or counterpoints. Tony Kushner doesn't make Zillah, who reads to herself silently, conflict with the large image projected behind her of a woman refusing to salute to Hitler in *A Bright Room Called Day*. When the play reaches the climax, words and image overlap for theatrical, thematic, aesthetic, and emotional effect.

It's possible for an audience to become accustomed to projected stills (such as silhouettes of trees) that provide backgrounds for characters without overwhelming unfolding action. As you imagine media usage, put yourself in the role of the audience and observe honestly the pros and cons of your choices. Video images take the audience's attention even more than stills. Video can be a powerful addition to a play, especially if your approach is multimedia and epic with a fractured action that deliberately at times diminishes individual characters. Some theatre companies use video as a main component in their work. However, any time a play relies on projections it runs the risk of technical troubles that might sabotage production.

Generally speaking, here are some pointers with regard to breaking the fourth wall:

- It's easier for an audience to remain emotionally absorbed in a drama if characters don't break the fourth wall. Even scene breaks briefly remind an audience that they're in a theatre, but people might find it easier to sustain the mood you want if they aren't addressed directly.
- Breaking the fourth wall helps an audience focus on themes. It doesn't necessarily prevent emotional connection, as *Our Town* and *Angels in America* attest, but it does interrupt that connection to highlight ideas and appeal to people intellectually.
- If your play covers multiple time periods and/or multiple groups of characters and plotlines, a narrator or several characters addressing the audience can bring coherence to many different dramatic concepts and guide the emotional focus. In *La Ronde* a narrator leads the audience from one couple to another as var-

ious characters take turns being the primary actor.

- Don't call on mediated images unless they truly are necessary for the overall effect of the play and you think carefully about how to weave them into the action.

WRITING EXERCISES FOR TODAY:

1. Will you break fourth wall illusion? If not, why not? If so, why and how? Be clear about why those decisions best serve your play.
2. Will you use mediated images? If so, why and how?

Until tomorrow,
Linda

DAY 25

"If you slow things down, you notice things you hadn't seen before."

—**ROBERT WILSON**

SLOW DOWN—AND FIND YOUR POINT OF VIEW

Hi Writers,

Sometimes your mind whirrs so wildly that you lose touch with basic feelings and observations you need to call upon to create plausible actions and reactions. Writing can become stressful instead of joyful. Slow down to fully inhabit your body and be present moment to moment with no pressure to do anything else. Imagine yourself when you finish your first draft. Feel whatever you think you'll feel. Keep that emotional "picture" close as you write.

While you are in this state of being present and slowed down, think about the *point of view* you will ask your audience to take as the play unfolds. Usually a story-based play with a main character asks us to experience the unfolding action from the point of view of the main character. In the familiar versions of Cinderella we encounter the wicked family members from Cinderella's point of view. It's possible to tell that story from the point of view of the Stepmother. As a writer you choose and manipulate the point of view.

Sometimes the primary point of view is that of the *omniscient* ("all-knowing") storyteller, who takes us into the points of view of various characters. All of the Ladies in *for colored girls* share their points of view so that no one's experience is privileged over others. As Narrator, *Our Town*'s Stage Manager mediates point of view by telling us about the town and its people, then stepping back to let the characters take focus.

Is the point of view through which we enter the play reliable or admirable? What do we make of Blanche DuBois, for instance, in *A Streetcar Named Desire*, since we learn early on she is prone to delusion and deception? *Richard III* is the central character in his drama; while we see the action through his eyes, we might not like him or agree with his choices. We can learn a great deal about human flaws by experiencing the points of view of flawed humans.

Brazilian director Augusto Boal's "Theatre of the Oppressed" taught people in crisis situations to use point of view to help themselves. First Boal directed villagers to arrange one another in tableaux that visually represented how they felt about the current community dilemma. Those tableaux gave a "picture" of crisis. Next Boal asked the villagers to create tableaux that represented them as they might appear if they could overcome their difficulties. When they could see the difference between the beginning and the end, they could imagine the steps it would take to move to that positive ending. In *Circle Mirror Transformation* by Annie Baker, acting teacher Marty arranges others in attitudinal poses typical of relationships within her family. Next each member of the class directs a personal familial tableau. This "shows" rather than "tells" key information about each character, much like Boal's technique.

As you write be grounded in your own point of view, precise about whose point of view is guiding the dramatic action, and sensitive to the audience's point of view.

WRITING EXERCISES FOR TODAY:

1. How do you want your audience to relate to the character or characters where point of view resides? Do you want us to have empathy, to be appalled, or . . . what? And why?

2. Using Boal's technique, imagine your main character or one of your main characters visually at the beginning. Describe the first seconds in which that character is presented to the audience. What does the audience see and what is the audience likely to think about that character? Envision that character in physical relation to other characters onstage at that moment. What would we learn simply from what we see?

3. Write a monologue for how that character is feeling in those first seconds—before speaking.

4. Write what other characters are feeling about the main character in those first seconds.

5. Use Boal's technique to imagine your main character at the end, the last time we see him/her. Imagine both from the audience point of view and the character's point of view.

6. If other characters are onstage at the end, how might their physical relationship to the main character appear to be different from what we saw at the beginning?

Until tomorrow,
Linda

DAY 26

*"The creation of interest and suspense (in their very
widest sense) . . . underlies all dramatic construction."*

—**MARTIN ESSLIN**

CONSTRUCTING THE BEGINNING

Hi Writers,

Either through an early inciting incident, or a MacGuffin and then an inciting incident, you will set in motion in the Beginning the action-re-action mechanism that will propel the play to its conclusion. Your characters will face choices that have high stakes for the major players. If your play is thematic, like *for colored girls* or Jane Wagner's *The Search for Signs of Intelligent Life in the Universe*, introduce the main theme(s) and tone in a lively manner that will intrigue the audience. Conclude the Beginning with something intriguing and surprising that *"hooks"* the audience. While the play's End somehow resolves the overall action, your Beginning does just the opposite—it sets up one or more dilemmas that characters must face. That teasing hook at the end of the Beginning makes the audience want to experience the conflicts and conversations you'll explore more fully in the Middle.

While you arrange the plot points for your Beginning section, imagine how they'll serve the need for variety. "Intensity" doesn't necessarily mean something loud or frantic. It is possible to have a very intense sequence between characters that glare at each other without words, or even people that sit side by side while another character pontificates. Usually intensity is achieved through emotional depth, suspenseful action and/or a plot twist. There is no "rule" for how and when you generate those intense moments, except for the general principle that the hook at the end of your Beginning should be more intense or focused than anything we've experienced so far in the play. It tells us there's more to come that we can't predict. You might begin slowly with an interaction that has little emotional intensity and build incrementally to that hook, which happens with *Clybourne Park*. Or you can start with an audience-grabbing sequence, drop back after that into a sequence that's less intense, and then drive the action to a higher pitch, which Suzan-Lori Parks does in *Topdog/ Underdog*.

It will help your scenario arrangement if you identify plot points in terms of complication or conflict and reaction, not just physical action. Instead of "she runs away," try "when Larry humiliates her, she runs away." Or, "Larry humiliates her with the story about the car wreck." You might even be able to break down that "humiliation" into separate points. Some plays are almost entirely verbal action. In August Strindberg's *The Stronger* a woman confronts her lover's wife. By merely listening and nonverbally responding to an extended monologue by the mistress, the wife emerges as the stronger of the two. Each rhetorical twist and turn is a plot point. As you prepare to write the first section of your play, analyze how the plot points can be arranged most effectively with variety and slowly building intensity towards a cliffhanging "hook" that will lead into the Middle.

The structures of Beginning, Middle, and End differ in part because each plays a different role in leading an audience through dramatic experience. They also differ from one another in intensity, pace, and tone because audiences need variety. Similarly, then, you'll vary intensity, pace and tone within each section.

WRITING EXERCISES FOR TODAY:

1. In a full-length play the Beginning is approximately 15-30 script pages. As you outline the scenario, estimate where you'll place the MacGuffin (if you have one) and inciting incident, as well as other key plot points.
2. What might happen at the end of the Beginning that will "hook" an audience into the next section? If you have several ideas, note all of them.
3. Will you introduce all of your characters in the Beginning or will you save any for later? Be sure you know why you are making the choice in dramatic and theatrical terms.
4. Be as clear as possible regarding what problems and choices your character(s) will face during the play. How are you introducing that early in the Beginning?
5. If you're creating a montage of thematic material—how will you introduce that to an audience and why do you believe that's the most effective theatrical choice?

6. Analyze the opening sequences of one or more plays in view of these principles of construction. You will find wide variety and general patterns.

Until tomorrow,
Linda

DAY 27

HENRY: *"What we're trying to do is write cricket bats, so that when we throw up an idea and give it a little knock, it might . . . travel . . ."*

—TOM STOPPARD, *The Real Thing*

WRITING CRICKET BATS—BEAT BY BEAT

Hi Writers,

The words above are from a longer speech: "This thing here, which looks like a wooden club, is actually several pieces of particular wood cunningly put together in a certain way so that the whole thing is sprung, like a dance floor." Plays are "cunningly put together" assemblages of elements you create in your own "particular" ways. The smallest pieces, commonly called "*beats*," give a play life as much as the larger elements such as inciting incidents. Beats are the atomic structure of plays. The word "beat" is nothing mysterious. It means "bit." Actors from Constantin Stanislavski's Moscow Art Theatre spoke the word with their Russian accents as they taught American actors in the early 20th century, so the word sounded like "beat."

You build a play beat by beat. A director and actors rehearse beats and units of beats as they assemble a scene. It's often said that beats are like paragraphs, but that's misleading. Often they overlap, interlink and interrupt in ways that an orderly essay doesn't. Like a paragraph, though, each beat usually has one topic and structural integrity. Through common topics, arguments, and transitions, beats link to form larger episodes/units and then whole scenes. You construct a play one bit of character action/reaction or one topic at a time, with a new "beat" beginning when a new topic is introduced or another character enters, or the intensity rachets up in a significant way. The beats string together to form *units* (some call these *episodes*). Usually a series of units forms a *scene*. A series of related beats might form an entire short scene. Some, but not all, plays link scenes to form "*acts*." Beats, units, episodes, scenes, acts—however you think of the bits and segments of your play, all have their own inner shapes and purposes.

A beat might continue an earlier topic or introduce a new one in a minor vein, but essentially the characters riff or argue about one thing for a moment before shifting to another topic or a variation on the same topic. Longer beats each take up a separate topic. A long beat usually lasts approximately half a page to a page of script. (One page of play script generally takes one to three minutes to perform.)

Shorter beats usually offer transitions from one beat into another. Brief beats between longer ones can introduce other topics to tease the audience and perhaps to foreshadow later events. Also, they can interrupt one topic to prolong audience interest. Quick changes in beats help give the play a sense of forward movement. Conversely, a series of longer beats might slow the tempo. Thinking musically, you determine the pace at any given moment. Beats that are interruptions can make a play more exciting. Characters argue about a topic that's crucial to the central action—then entrances, exits, phone calls, extraneous events interrupt the flow with brief beats. Sometimes people deflect and deliberately go off topic to avoid continuing. This builds suspense and keeps the audience hooked.

At times a beat is about exploring characters' relationships and feelings more than driving the action forward. Those beats help the audience feel more invested in the characters' emotional journeys, which enriches the ending. Character development beats tend to work better in the Middle of the play, after you've already established the action.

The Watchman's speech in the opening (prologos) of *Agamemnon* is one long series of related and uninterrupted beats. He bemoans having spent a year on the palace roof watching, tells of stars he's followed through seasons, then explains Clytemnestra ordered him to watch for a beacon signaling Troy has been captured. Next he confides that he cannot sleep for fear and cries because this home is in trouble. As he prays for change, the beacon light appears in the distance. Excited, he must send news. This speech ends with a foreshadowing of the action to come: "This house if it could talk would tell a tale." Aeschylus gives each thought a separate beat. Drawn into the Watchman's feelings, the audience can hear each distinctly. This one short scene sets up drama with linear elegance.

Consider the beats in the opening of Steve Totland's *You Are Here*, on the following pages. These pages also illustrate conventional script formatting, minus the lines denoting beat divisions. You might see the beats slightly differently. Observe that Totland gives beats "breathing room" for the audience to fully take in the action. The first beat is a silent moment that gives the audience time to see evidence of someone studying and depictions of donuts and milk as well as other oddities. We are intrigued. When an alarm's ring begins the second beat we are astounded to see a man rise from clothes on the sofa. He disentangles himself in an intriguing short beat. The next beat is longer and more complex as Roger marks off on a chart and calls off, "Once upon a time." Again, we realize something odd is happening and want to understand this situation. In succeeding beats Roger knocks on the wall and Clarice enters the mix. All the characters behave as if everything that happens is perfectly normal in their world, while it is slightly skewed for us. In one long beat we learn it's Wednesday morning, Roger "got nerves" and Clarice assures him, "You'll do fine." Otherwise, there is no information given directly to the audience. The writer immerses us in Roger's anxiety, beat by beat.

WRITING EXERCISES FOR TODAY:

1. Describe the important beats in your Beginning.
2. Can a speech or interchange you want in the Beginning be a series of smaller beats?
3. Practice "breaking down" scenes of familiar plays into beats. Look at plays you have at home. Study how the beats are shaped, especially those in the Beginning, how they interact, how they build to comprise a unified sequence.

Until tomorrow,
Linda

ONE

Late February. Wednesday. Early morning.

Roger and Guy's apartment.

In the living room a worn sofa and arm chair. In front of the sofa, a coffee table covered with three-ring binders, training manuals, organizational flow charts. An end table with a lamp and alarm clock.

Taped to the wall over the sofa are glossy posters detailing standards for glazing donuts and steaming milk. Also, a hand-crafted poster for registering the completion of daily chores.

To one side of the living room is a dining table covered with school texts, pencils, loose-leaf paper, a calculator, a well-worn backpack.

A kitchen off the dining area.

A hallway leads from the living room to the apartment's one bedroom and bathroom.

Mounds of clothes scattered across the sofa and chair. An empty clothes basket near the coffee table.

Quiet.

The alarm rings.

Roger, who has been sleeping on the sofa amidst the clothes, bolts upright.

ROGER

[Loud.] Alarm! Time to get up!

Roger turns off the alarm.

He disentangles himself from the clothes; sits.

He turns to the wall; uses a marker to make a big X in a box on his chore chart.

He sits. /// Then,

ROGER (cont'd)

[Calling off.] "Once upon a time. . ."

He listens for a response.

ROGER (cont'd)

[Calling off.] "Once upon a time. . ."

He listens.

Silence.

Roger walks to the hallway.

ROGER (cont'd)

[Calling into the hallway.] "Once upon a time. . ."

Roger listens.

[Louder.] "Once upon a time. . ."

Finally, from off, a low, rumbling groan.

ROGER (cont'd)

[Calling off.] Guy!

GUY

[Off. Nearly intelligible.] I hear you.

Roger listens; hears nothing more.

He returns to the sofa; sits.

Roger turns; knocks "shave and a haircut" onto the wall behind the sofa. Immediately, "two bits' comes back from the other side of the wall.

ROGER

[Speaking into the wall.] 'Morning, Clarice.

CLARICE

[From the other side of the wall.] 'Morning, Roger.

ROGER

Just a minute, Clarice.

Roger crosses back to the hallway door.

ROGER (cont'd)

[Calling off.] Guy.

GUY

[Off.] I'm awake.

ROGER

[Calling off.] Time flies.

Roger crosses back to the sofa. He and Clarice continue speaking to each other from opposite sides of the wall.

ROGER (cont'd)

I'm back.

CLARICE

Wednesday morning.

ROGER

Easy to know that. Everywhere you look the clothes are clean. How'd you sleep?

CLARICE

Like a baby.

ROGER

I was tossy-turny. I got nerves.

CLARICE

You'll do fine.

ROGER

That's what they say.

DAY 28

"Is it possible for those of us exploring our various crafts
to understand and accept the idea that all of us are on
a sacred journey? A quest to discover the divine in our
work, in our world, and in ourselves?"
—MARY SCRUGGS & MICHAEL J. GELLMAN

PREPARING TO BEGIN THE DRAFT

Hi Writers,

You'll begin the first beats of the Beginning tomorrow. Writers help their
audiences connect with dreams and feelings not articulated. Part of your
daily preparation, then, is to set yourself free to go into the farthest corners of your spirit.

As you finish drafting a rough scenario before you launch into writing
tomorrow, here are more principles to help you with the broad outlines
of the Middle and End: In the Middle centripetal force comes into play.
There will be a blossoming or dynamic explosion of actions/reactions and
themes resulting from your set up. This will help you keep the audience
believing there are multiple ways the characters might conclude their drama. If you aren't constructing a story, your themes gain greater depth and
dimension in the Middle. For the End, forces set loose in the Middle come
to a head (crisis) requiring decisions, the action focuses (climax), and a
conclusion emerges as centrifugal force takes over. If you're working with
an assemblage that isn't story-based you merge thematic/visual/linguistic
components.

Do you have a *title* for your play? Writers commonly begin with one
title and then shift to another as the play emerges. Most titles refer to
action, theme or both. Many plays take their titles from the name of the
main character, whose actions and fate define the story. *Bug* is a provocative title; its layered meaning emerges by play's end. *Topdog/Underdog*
suggests the endless loop of dominance/subjugation that typifies much of
human experience. Like sketching loglines, fabricating titles might help
you focus on the way forward tomorrow.

WRITING EXERCISES FOR TODAY:

1. Tie up preliminary loose ends for your scenario and plot logic.
2. What title or titles might you give this play and why?
3. Review your logline/action statement and the plot points you have for the spine of action.
4. Remember why you want to write this particular play. What excites you? What has meaning for you? What themes, relationships and conflicts do you want to explore in writing this?
5. Study your scenario for the Beginning, especially the opening beats—do you have what you need to write tomorrow? If not, reflect on the questions you have for the Beginning.
6. Review what you want to accomplish in your writing tomorrow—make sure it's a manageable goal you can face with confidence. Go over the specifics of the opening you imagine—the beats, the theatricality, the characters' feelings. See it. Feel their emotions.
7. Now sleep and set the inner worker free.

Until tomorrow,
Linda

WEEK 4: THOUGHTS AND REMINDERS

- Beat by beat you build a unit of action, an active scene, a drama.

- Prepare to begin writing. Review the elements you've assembled—remember why they're needed and why you've chosen them—or make a note if you haven't decided.
  - Logline/Action Statement
  - Dramatic Action / Spine / Throughline
  - Working Title
  - Protagonist or Ensemble
  - Antagonist(s) / Confidant(s)-Allies / Counterpoints
  - Character ideas, voices, plot points
  - Theatricality—ideas for characters
  - Theme(s)
  - Point of Attack—as close to the end of your story as possible
  - Point of View
  - Inciting Incident
  - MacGuffin
  - Beginning / Middle / End
  - Plot points in a rough Scenario
  - The end of the Beginning
  - Hooks for the audience
  - Fourth Wall—break it or not?
  - Framing Devices
  - Narrator
  - Mediated Images

- Every play has a Beginning, Middle, and End—and every play constructs those differently while following some basic principles.

- Your Beginning sets up the play—you invite your audience into a game by catching their interest and showing the "rules."

- Consider the technique of Augusto Boal—see your characters at the Beginning and the End.

- Remember why you're writing a play—this play.

- Practice slowing down to be present in the moment with your characters.

- Commit to beginning to draft your play tomorrow—beat by beat.

UNIT TWO

WRITING THE BEGINNING

You will write each day through the scenario you've devised. At the end of three weeks you will prepare for beginning work on the play's Middle section. Your play is becoming concrete and vivid as you compress dramatic time, devise language tactics, and explore decisions your characters must make.

WEEK 5

BEGINNING THE BEGINNING

This week you commit to creating the play's opening moments and set up the rules of the game for the audience. You make decisions about the dramatic time the play requires, how you'll treat exposition, and effective use of entrances and exits.

DAY 29

"Just do it."

—CHOGYAM TRUNGPA RINPOCHE

GET SET, GO

Hi Writers,

Today you begin creating your play from the first moment, fitting together the logic and patterns you imagine while remaining open to surprises. You do the best you can and commit to forward movement each day without self-censoring. Letters and exercises help you write through your scenario in sequence. However, you will continue to imagine scenes, images, monologues and dialogue out of sequence—creativity is more associative than linear. Write everything that comes as your imagination flows while adhering to the discipline of writing through the play as it would unfold onstage. Let the scenario change as needed.

You'll write the Middle in Unit Three and complete the play in Unit Four. I suggest you stop at the end of each unit to review and tweak as well as plan scenario and corrections. However, if you're inspired and don't want to stop, don't. You might write half a page one day, three the next. You could be on a roll, charging through the Beginning without halting. Or, perhaps you're "stuck" for a few days. If you average 1.5 pages a day you'll have 90 pages at the end of this course. If you're writing a shorter play you can draft and rewrite it in this time.

The quote above from a Buddhist master is a good mantra for us all. Sometimes you won't be able to write a scene you have in mind. However, you can always work on the play. I attended a lecture by Trungpa Rinpoche (d. 1987) in Evanston, Illinois. After calming the audience, he asked for questions. A young woman rambled about trying to do something but not knowing how to begin. He smiled at her with objective compassion and replied, "Just do it." There really isn't anything else. In the time it takes to come up with an excuse for why you aren't writing, you can create at least one beat, one exchange of dialogue, one monologue. You will build the "muscles" for writing.

SUGGESTIONS FOR THE DAY:

1. Write on a page separate from the script your cast of characters (dramatis personae), with brief descriptions of each one that includes their ages and relationships to one another.
2. Describe each setting you imagine for the play on a separate page. If these are only vague for you right now, that's fine.
3. Write the opening of the play, aim for the first page or two. If you aren't certain how to begin—and it's normal not to know—try the possibilities. Before you begin, take time to fully situate yourself in the opening scene. See, hear and sense it the way your characters will. Be there with them. Begin.
4. Reflect in your personal journal on what you've learned by beginning.

Until tomorrow,
Linda

HOMEWORK FOR THE WEEK

1. Write through the opening unit or scene of your play.

2. Do the daily writing exercises.

3. Work with exercises at the back of the book as appropriate and needed.

4. Reflect in your personal journal on what you're learning.

DAY 30

*"A play is not a flat work of literature, not a description
in poetry of another world, but in itself another world
passing before you in time and space."*

—**ELINOR FUCHS**

DRAMATIC TIME

Hi Writers,

Your play is happening in the semblance of "real time," not in real time itself. *Dramatic time* is selected, compressed and efficient. Although the point of attack will be as close as possible to the conclusion of the play, the action can occur over weeks, even years. The audience should feel the play takes no more time than is necessary to convey the drama. *Oedipus the King* seems to take place in one day: Messengers come and go, action intensifies, inevitability takes over, characters meet crisis, the Queen kills herself, and the King resolves the plague by blinding himself and going into exile—all in one "stage day." It's hardly credible that so much could happen in one actual day. Some critics took Aristotle's description of a lovely play literally and decided all good plays should happen in one day. Throw that rule out the window. Shakespeare did. So did Chekhov and Arthur Miller. The "rules" are about plausibility, compression and urgency.

Breaks between scenes for time passage or change of setting might interrupt the audience's connection to the action. To keep them in your play time, end the beat just before the interruption with an intriguing hook or teaser. A *hook* is unresolved dissonance that is crucial enough for the audience to want to know how it will be addressed. This can be as simple as a disagreement between characters left unsettled. The audience will accept the leap in time when the next beat begins.

Stage time can "bend" in various ways. A play can intercut past and present to illuminate both. "Realistic" time can open into "dream time." *Flashbacks* are scenes from the past that suddenly appear in the play's present time. Use these variations on time only if they are the best way to convey events, if they are consistent with your style and logic, and if they keep the sense of forward momentum for your play. They can provide a significant dimension such as having Emily revisit her past in *Our Town*.

Ideally, a flashback to something that occurred prior to your point of attack will reveal something interesting about the past while at the same time dropping in additional information, the seed of something unresolved, that makes an audience want to know what will happen in the future. You can plant a mystery or secret in flashback that will propel action in the present and generate suspense. John Guare's *Landscape of the Body* moves in and out of past and present fluidly, like a dream, circling the agonizing question of how and why a boy died. The play's form is perfectly suited to themes about the slippery nature of love, truth and memory. Scenes that move backwards in time can confuse, disorient, or, even worse, bore an audience if they exist only to explain the past.

The dramatic time you choose should fit your idea, action, characters, style, and desired effect. *Boy Gets Girl* needs weeks for Tony's stalking to escalate. *Who's Afraid of Virginia Woolf?* takes place from 2 a.m. to dawn, slightly longer in "real" time than in stage time. If you can compress the number of hours, days or weeks you're allowing for the action, do so. The tighter the time, the greater the sense of urgency for characters and audience. Don't be afraid to compress dramatic time drastically. But don't do it because of Aristotle.

SUGGESTIONS FOR THE DAY:

1. How much "real time" have you planned for your scenario? How little can you select and still keep the plot plausible? Sketch into your scenario the "real time" you think is happening from unit to unit, scene to scene.
2. Sketch possible hooks as plot points before time breaks into your scenario.

Until tomorrow,
Linda

DAY 31

"Exposition is any information in the play about circumstances that precede the beginning, occur offstage, or happen between scenes."

—Sam Smiley

EXPOSITION

Hi Writers,

Exposition is another way to create drama and intrigue instead of merely something that has to be told. Save it for moments of anger, confusion, or trust. Let it be something a character bottles up and blurts out under pressure. Use it to surprise the audience, to provide a hook at the end of a sequence of beats. Let it be the topic that creates argument. As often as possible, show rather than tell us expository information. Characters usually give us through words most of the information we need about them and their story in order to understand the unfolding drama. Sometimes physical action and gestures convey exposition; for example, the way characters greet one another implies the nature of their relationship. But rather than be merely "expository," in a play that seems "realistic" that information should be incorporated into what people must say to or do with one another and into what is appropriate at that moment.

There are theatrically effective ways to use exposition to your advantage instead of thinking of it as an obligation. If your play uses direct address to the audience, media, a narrator, or other such devices, those devices can deliver exposition directly to an audience. Even then, though, the audience should believe what they're being told is important for them to understand at that moment and necessary to enjoy the action to come. Also, the narration itself should be entertaining in some manner. Study the Stage Manager in *Our Town* for an example of well-crafted direct address exposition that is more than the mere sharing of information.

You have created a rich dramatic world for your characters. Some information about a character's background might inform you but doesn't fit logically or aesthetically into the script. For example, the characters in

Red don't talk about Rothko's previous work, Ken's training, what year it is, their personal lives outside the studio, and so forth. Ken's parents' deaths are a key to their discussion about color and emotions—otherwise Ken's family is not mentioned. On the other hand, August Wilson's characters swap stories about people they know and places they've been to create a dramatic world onstage. We experience the past that is informing the present in his characters' conflicts. In *The Piano Lesson*, for instance, Boy Willie argues with his sister over the ownership of a piano that carries both family and African-American history. He argues with references to stories they both know—to vivify shared lives and dreams.

Information the audience needs but the characters already know usually is the most difficult to convey. Why would characters mention something they already know? Find an active way to place that information—through characters in argument or teasing, in a confession, and so forth. "You remember Ken, I dated him before I met Ollie." "Yes, I remember Ken, he dumped me to date you." "I didn't know that." "Well, now you do." Or it might be tossed off: "She'll be here, don't worry, she's always late. She probably missed her flight."

From the outset *Topdog/Underdog* signals us to expect a kind of hyper-reality, the appearance of realism but a story and characters that operate as fable, metaphor, or symbol. Two brothers recall the one little house they shared with their parents. They both know this information, so why repeat it? Their memory is conveyed to the audience in shared dialogue: Once upon a time we had a house and we were a family. While this might be exposition for the audience, it also operates like a ritual for the abandoned, destitute brothers.

It's easier if one character needs to know something another already knows. You still have to find the place and way to convey it for maximum dramatic and theatrical impact, or at the very least so the audience will be sure to hear and remember it.

You might be tempted to place most of your exposition in the Beginning, thinking an audience needs to know all your information in the "set up" of the play. However, that can burden your Beginning. Instead, plunge an audience into a situation with characters in action. Give an audience time to become curious before telling them much that is expository. We're well into *Uncle Vanya* before we understand all the characters' relationships. Sonya calls Vanya "Uncle," but how is he her uncle? The Professor is staying there with his wife Elena—who are they to Vanya and this household? Since the characters know all this, Chekhov immerses us in their world and takes his time. These relationships finally become clear when the Professor wants to sell the estate; at crisis we grasp Sonya's story and her centrality in Vanya's survival.

Give as little information as you believe absolutely necessary in your initial writing. When you rewrite you'll see more clearly exactly what is needed and where it can best be placed in the action so it has the most impact and fits with the flow. Some information is so important that it needs to be repeated for the audience and/or characters. Look for the organic moments. Wait until a rewrite if you can't figure out how to convey the information in this draft.

SUGGESTIONS FOR THE DAY:

1. Create a separate list of information that must be conveyed, if you haven't already. Does anyone need to know that Julie used to be a doctor? How important is it that we know the exact year when the protagonist was divorced, there's a wedding tomorrow, etc.?
2. Separate the information into categories: 1) Information the audience needs to know but one or more characters already know; 2) information one or more characters need to learn (be specific about which characters need this, why, and when); 3) information audience and characters need to know.
3. Note what information is absolutely vital to the plot or texture of the play.

Until tomorrow,
Linda

DAY 32

*"I write plays because writing dialogue is the only
respectable way of contradicting yourself. I put a position,
rebut it, refute the rebuttal, and rebut the refutation."*
                                        —TOM STOPPARD

POINT / COUNTERPOINT

Hi Writers,

Today's letter is the first of many addressing dramatic language. By definition *dialogue* is "two" speakers, but in theatrical practice it refers to more
than one speaker engaging with one another in multiple ways. Varying
the nature of your characters' dialogue adds spice to the entertainment
and points the audience to important themes. A "classical" approach to
dialogue is a *point/counterpoint* exchange between or among characters
that is an argument in which people stay on a topic to parry and thrust,
contradicting and refuting one another in a word duel. Some plays use
this throughout; others, only a little. Bernard Shaw, Noel Coward and
Stoppard use argumentative dialogue frequently while Horton Foote rarely employs the device.

"*Stichomythia*" is an ancient form of point/counterpoint. In stichomythia the second speaker picks up the wording and rhythm from the
previous speaker and twists it. Here Gertrude refers to Hamlet's new
"father," his uncle Claudius, while Hamlet refers to his biological father,
whom he believes was slain by Claudius:

> GERTRUDE: Hamlet, thou hast thy father much offend-
> ed.
> HAMLET: Mother, you have my father much offended.

Point/counterpoint or *thesis/antithesis* construction, whether or not it
is stichomythia, usually works best when used sparingly and strategically.
When characters cease longer interchanges that are less argumentative to
launch a tit for tat duel, it catches the audience's attention because it's as if
the play has suddenly become more intensely focused. The writer creates

a verbal duel, a contest of ideas. The technique helps us understand how hard a character will fight for an idea and how well characters understand each other's position. Marsha Norman uses this duel between mother and daughter for comic as well as tragic effect in 'night, Mother. Generally speaking, point/counterpoint exchanges don't last long; having caught the audience, the writer can then give one of the characters a monologue containing ideas or revelations that deserve highlighting.

Red uses point/counterpoint in a key moment for emphasis. As Rothko's assistant, Ken hesitates to cross the artist. Following their dialogue through the five scenes, we watch Rothko challenge Ken to argue while assuming superiority. Ken avoids crossing his temperamental boss. The men go toe to toe in Scene 4 as the action moves into crisis. Ken asserts himself, referring to Rothko's plan to place his paintings in the Four Seasons.

> KEN: At least Andy Warhol gets the joke.
> ROTHKO: No, you don't understand.
> KEN: It's a fancy restaurant in a big high rise owned by a rich corporation, what don't I understand?
> ROTHKO: You don't understand my intention.
> KEN: Your intention is immaterial. . . . The art has to speak for itself, yes?
> ROTHKO: Yes, but—
> KEN: Just admit your hypocrisy. . . . You rail against commercialism in art, but pal, you're taking the money.
>
> Longer exchanges along these lines ensue, then—
>
> ROTHKO: You think it's all an act of monumental self-delusion. . . . Answer me.
> KEN: Yes. . . . I'm fired, aren't I?
> ROTHKO: Fired? . . . . This is the first time you've existed.

If you study the form of their dialogue from beginning to end you can see their changing relationship and the climax, the turning point, when the younger generation achieves parity with, and possibly begins to surpass, the old.

Euripides uses this rhetorical device in a different way and place in *The Bacchae*. Disguised, the god Dionysus attempts to persuade rigid ruler Pentheus that Thebes should be allowed to worship Dionysus. With song and honeyed words, Dionysus's chorus shows Pentheus all that is good about the god of nature. "Rational" Pentheus won't be swayed. Exactly midway through the play, Dionysus confronts him in spare point/counterpoint that ends with this:

> PENTHEUS: But I say: chain him. And I am the
> stronger here.
> DIONYSUS: You do not know the limits of your
> strength. You do not know what you do. You do not
> know who you are.
> PENTHEUS: I am Pentheus, the son of Echion and
> Agave.
> DIONYSUS: Pentheus: you shall repent that name.

With that the action turns 180 degrees. The god punishes Pentheus's entire family for refusing to recognize the force of nature as divine.

SUGGESTIONS FOR THE DAY:

1. Will you use point/counterpoint in your play? Which characters? When? Why?
2. Have characters use this argumentative style of dialogue. They might argue over, for example, politics, a popular film, the placement of a chair in the room, vegetarianism.
3. If a character speaks for you, place that character with one who contradicts him/her vigorously. Challenge yourself with the opposite of your beliefs.

Until tomorrow,
Linda

DAY 33

*"People ask me when I decided to become a playwright,
and I tell them I decide to do it every day. Most days
it's very hard because I'm frightened—not frightened of
writing a bad play, although that happens often with me.
I'm frightened of encountering the wilderness of my own
spirit."*

—SUZAN-LORI PARKS

LOOK BACK, GO FORWARD

Hi Writers,

Easing into writing time can be difficult, largely because your body and mind are still "in" whatever you were doing earlier. Often you need time to integrate yourself and turn your focus to the specific writing you intend to do on a given day. If you sit down and think, "Now I'll work on my play," chances are you'll have difficulty beginning. That in turn can deceive you into thinking you're "blocked." Try this warmup technique:

Review the scenario to remind yourself where you want to begin today. If you have a plan for this next unit of beats or an entire scene—what is it?

Review what you wrote yesterday—possibly several pages or scenes before where you need to begin today. Your goal should not be to revise it. You are getting into the dramatic world, the characters and style, and thinking into the point in the plot where you stopped before. Hear the characters. Inhabit their feelings.

Now return to thinking about today's work. If there's no plan for it, at least be clear about where you were yesterday and spur imagination with plot questions. What should be the action today? What's the problem to work out? What challenge will be introduced? Also—do you want to vary the next scene by making it humorous where yesterday's was serious, quiet instead of raucous, building suspense or taking a break in the suspense?

When you've taken time to immerse your imagination in the play, you should be ready to write. Now put yourself on the stage, in the scene with the characters. Be in the moment—think only about that first beat. Who will speak or act first? Embody that character, hear his/her voice. Pretend you are that character. Go.

This method, or a variation on it that works for you, provides a transition into creative thought and productive writing; offers a ritual/habit that gives your imagination guidance and permission to fly; helps ensure character and plot consistency; helps you create variety—a new scene with a new rhythm, contrast or complement to what came before.

SUGGESTIONS FOR THE DAY:

Try the process above while you continue to write the Beginning.

Until tomorrow,
Linda

DAY 34

"It is a truism of ancient stagecraft that the one who controls the doorway controls the tragedy, according to Oliver Taplin."

—ANNE CARSON

COMING AND GOING

Hi Writers,

It's tempting while writing a play to think mainly of what characters say. However, the audience sees everything on stage. When a character enters or leaves a scene, all eyes are on that character. And if all eyes are on a character—how do you adjust to it? Moreover, how do you make the most of it? Clytemnestra controls the entry into her palace like no other character in drama ever has controlled a doorway. She stands between her returning husband Agamemnon and that entry—his palace, but now her domain and the site of his impending murder.

For the beginning of *The Pillowman*, Martin McDonagh combines a mysterious initial image with an entrance that sets up audience expectation for action. The play opens on a blindfolded man seated at a table. Next two men enter and sit opposite him; one has a file with papers. When the other two enter our eyes swing to them but also want to keep watching the blindfolded man. Before a word is spoken the audience takes in the entire scene and suspects this will be a familiar police interrogation—which will prove to be only partially true.

Don't have important dialogue or action occurring onstage while another character enters or exits. The entrance/exit will interrupt and the audience won't hear what's said. Use the interruption for theatrical effect, perhaps to suspend a confrontation that the audience will want to return to. Even if a character slides through the doorway and the other characters don't see him/her, the audience will. If the other characters are saying anything important to your plot or theme, the audience will miss it. All eyes go to the one sliding in. "The one who controls the doorway" almost always will control audience attention. As a corollary, usually allow for a brief moment before a character who enters says anything important (unless they're in a rush, calling for help, for example). The audience is seeing what's happening and can't always take in what's being said at the same time.

Usually each time a character enters or leaves, others onstage react to that. If they don't, if they ignore the person entering or exiting, that should be germane to your action. The audience expects reactions. This is a useful opportunity to insert important information and ideas, because the audience is paying attention. The reaction or lack of it should contribute to the ongoing drama and help us better know your characters.

Describe comings and goings in stage directions. Does Lou bang open the door and rush in, out of breath, rather than simply "enter"? Does Marie stride in without invitation, glaring at anyone in particular? And how do they leave? Is Jared reluctant, afraid to turn his back to the others? Does Felicia square her shoulders and take a breath before facing the unknown? Then—how do other characters react to these people? Does each one on stage have a different reaction? Is one saddened while another says, "Good riddance"? If you want to leave it to a director to decide how characters will enter and exit, it helps nevertheless to write in your first draft exactly what you see. You can edit that later.

Always know where a character is coming from before s/he enters. Characters don't enter and exit because it's convenient for the playwright. Why has s/he come to this place? Why enter the scene and with what attitude? The character wants or needs something—what is it and how does s/he intend to get it? Conversely, why is the character leaving and where is s/he going?

Entrances and exits mark beginnings and endings of beats, units and whole scenes. Something new is added, something in the action changes with each coming or going. Some writers construct plays in "French scenes." That is, each time there is an addition to or subtraction from characters onstage a new scene begins. Each new scene is given a number. This convention in classical French plays can be useful because it helps you track characters' movements. You can always delete the numbers in rewrites if you prefer a continuous flow.

Entrances and exits can support the spine of a play. In Act I of *Clybourne Park* we begin with the main character, Russ, and his wife Bev. One by one a character enters who'll participate in the play's crisis and climax, though at first we can't imagine how that will happen. We meet each one and watch them fold into Russ and Bev's plan to move. Antagonist Lindner comes into this scene late, so everyone can react to him and prepare us for crisis. Kenneth, the son who committed suicide, enters after the Act II climax. In military uniform, he descends the staircase from the room where he killed himself and takes a seat onstage. With his entrance the play's theme assumes prominence: History matters and permeates the present.

Consider teasing an entrance so the audience eagerly anticipates seeing a character. By the time Tartuffe appears in Moliere's play by that title we have heard so much about him that we can hardly wait to encounter him in person. Similarly, August Wilson has white producers and black band members talk about Ma Rainey so we know she will rule the roost when she appears, and indeed she enters with a flourish, commanding everyone's obedience.

SUGGESTIONS FOR THE DAY:

1. Be specific, inventive and effective with each character's entrance and exit. Why this choice?

2. Where is each character coming from or going to with each entry/exit? Why?
3. Leaf through plays you have on hand to study a variety of approaches to comings and goings.

Until tomorrow,
Linda

DAY 35

"Drama . . . is to a very considerable extent concerned with . . . letting audiences partake in emotions that would otherwise be denied them, and is a means of widening their experience as human beings."

—Martin Esslin

DECISIONS, DECISIONS

Hi Writers,

In theatre we experience how other people react to problems and dilemmas—how they argue and make sense of things—and how they make decisions. Whether they make decisions logically and well or not, whether the results are happy or tragic or somewhere in between, we learn from others and we feel with them. Because decisions are at the heart of drama there are several important ways to think about them: where they fit in the structure, how they are integral to characterization and relationships, and how they're revealed to other characters and the audience.

As you write the Beginning, your characters might face significant decisions. Sometimes the inciting incident that sets the drama in motion is a decision made—usually by the main character. A decision might establish the point of attack. Another decision can end the Beginning section in a way that turns the action in new directions. Decisions made in the Beginning reveal characters' personalities and modes of thinking. Reactions to them by other characters help us understand all the characters. Early decisions characters make propel the action by generating the need for confrontation, solutions and resolutions. Decisions made in the Beginning do not resolve the action—they spur it on.

Usually important decisions are made onstage because the audience wants to experience how your characters think, how they react to a problem and analyze what must be done. Jocasta kills herself offstage, which keeps the focus on her husband Oedipus's reaction to that and the decision he makes onstage. A woman announces she intends to kill herself in the beginning of Marsha Norman's 'night Mother. Will that decision hold? Can her mother persuade her not to? The action of the play reveals why she made that decision and why she will stick to it.

In Scott McPherson's *Marvin's Room* a woman with cancer has asked her estranged sister and nephews to visit the sisters' dying father because she needs them to be tested for a bone marrow donation. Each one struggles with whether or not to honor her request. The decisions each must make and the effects those have on the others propel the action. Widowed young Marlene refuses to take money from the company responsible for her husband's death in *Mill Fire*, and she doesn't want to attend the memorial that company is holding for workers who died in a suspicious fire. Writer Sally Nemeth gives us Marlene's decisions early in the play so we and other characters must understand her reasoning, experience her grief, watch others attempt to make her change her mind, and finally see events from her perspective.

Decisions in the Middle tighten the focus but still keep multiple endings possible. A decision at the end of the Middle might propel us into the End. Decisions at the End are the most important ones in your drama. They matter the most to your characters and have the greatest emotional impact for the audience. They carry thematic ideas more than others. They spur crisis and lead to climax, and they can conclude the story.

Let us fully experience your characters' decisions with them, onstage. Make sure we know how and why those decisions were made. That's why we're in your audience.

SUGGESTIONS FOR THE DAY:

1. What are the important decisions to be made in your play? Who must make them? Why?
2. When would be best for these decisions to be shared with the audience?

Until tomorrow,
Linda

WEEK 5: THOUGHTS AND REMINDERS

- Write beat by beat as you begin the Beginning.

- Be present with your characters and audience, moment by moment.

- Write out your list of characters with brief descriptions.

- Write your set descriptions.

- Consider creating point/counterpoint dialogue for strategic reasons and as appropriate to characters.

- Theatrical truth need only *seem* credible.

- The dramatic time of your play should be as condensed and efficient as possible.

- If the action breaks between units or scenes, end before the break with a "hook" that will make the audience curious to see what happens next.

- Use only the exposition that is *necessary* for the audience and/ or characters.

- Keep the Beginning moving forward with very little exposition.

- Exposition should help create drama and intrigue.

- Each day before you write, review your scenario and the beats, unit, or scene before what you plan today so the next writing will be consistent and logical.

- Each day as you begin, be centered in the moment of the beat you are about to write. Embody the character who will speak.

- Play with entrances and exits, comings and goings—use these for dramatic moments and to support the spine.

- The audience will look at who is entering and who is leaving more than they will listen to characters.

- Once the play has begun, reveal key moments of decision onstage.

- Audiences want to share characters' reactions and emotions—take time for those onstage.

WEEK 6

THEATRICALITY AND INCITEMENT

You are creating dramatic intrusions that ignite action and you practice being fully "present" in each beat. Your characters speak tactically and from necessity. You learn to use silence as effective technique.

DAY 36

*"Dramatic intrusion is the thing that comes along and
happens, setting free the irresistible forces that run a play
from that point on."*

—**DAVID BALL**

DRAMATIC INTRUSION / INCITING INCIDENTS

Hi Writers,

A *dramatic intrusion* is an event or information that propels a play forward in a particular direction. The inciting incident is the first intrusion.
Significant incidents—dramatic intrusions—propel characters into actions, reactions, and decisions. The Beginning should contain an incident
that sets free "irresistible forces that run the play from that point on" and
end with suspense about what will follow. You can begin with an inciting
incident and then create another—a hook—at the transition of Beginning
into Middle. Or, you can begin with a MacGuffin and save the inciting
incident for later.

   If you are interweaving multiple storylines, make one storyline dominant and begin early with an intrusion that sets it into motion. *The Taming
of the Shrew* begins with a father's desire to wed his compliant younger
daughter, but his older shrewish daughter Kate must by tradition marry
first. A crude suitor's proposal to marry Kate is the major intrusion that
informs the drama. Kate's is the dominant storyline because conflict and
suspense reside in it; the younger daughter's is secondary. A minor third
storyline echoes issues in the first two. These three interweave, intersect,
and interrupt one another, but the taming of the shrew dominates the
action. In the end, all three resolve with the dominant characters holding
center stage.

Don't spur action in all of the plotlines at once; let each come to a boil in different ways at different times as they braid in and out, using intrusions to thrust them in new directions. They shine light on one another as they reflect the main themes. End scenes with suspenseful hooks as you shift from one line to another. Arthur Schnitzler's *La Ronde* is, as the title suggests, a round dance. We begin with one couple and then follow one member of that couple as s/he moves on to another coupling. As one might in a group dance, characters change partners. With each intrusive change a new set of problems and decisions occur. The "dance" structure resolves, returning us to initial characters. Everyone's life has changed due to encounters with others.

Angels in America provides an excellent example of a contemporary multiple plot structure. Tony Kushner quickly introduces main character Prior Walter and the play's problem: Prior has AIDS (in the early years when few knew what it was). Kushner layers in multiple storylines involving Prior's lover Louis; Louis's quandaries and encounters with others; closeted Mormon Joe, his wife, his boss and his mother; and additional characters "real," historical and imaginary, including an Angel that crashes in through Prior's ceiling. With a variety of surprising intrusions, the throughlines intersect and influence each other. Often the stage splits, with scenes from two plots occurring simultaneously. As tension builds, some characters walk in and out of the plots in dream or fantasy sequences. While keeping Prior prominent, Kushner plays with numerous couplings among characters driven by variations on desire and power, anchored by the theme of a society facing the advent of AIDS.

For a play that isn't story-based you create intrusions that shake up the status quo, surprise your audience, and create aesthetic momentum. Those intrusions might be in the form of stark contrasts between scenes in tone, theatricality and/or theme that generate friction, more like a symphony than a story. The audience wonders how these contrasts will accelerate or continue to inform each other as well as surprise and intrigue us.

SUGGESTIONS FOR THE DAY:

1. Review scenario planning for the inciting incident and the intrusion and/or hook that will mark the end of your Beginning. Keep that end goal in mind as you create the beats, units, and scenes leading up to it.

2. Are the dramatic intrusions you have in mind consistent with character and story logic?

3. Are they occurring in an organic fashion (i.e., make sure you aren't forcing them)?

4. Are you thinking about all the possible reactions by your characters to those intrusions?

Until tomorrow,
Linda

HOMEWORK FOR THE WEEK

1. Continue writing the Beginning, giving special consideration to intrusions and theatricality.

2. Continue imagining and collecting in stream-of-consciousness.

3. Read aloud what you've written to help you slow down, take time, be "present."

DAY 37

"Stay in the moment. Make discoveries."

—MARY SCRUGGS

TAKING YOUR TIME

Hi Writers,

Mary Scruggs's advice may seem too simple. After all, you have pages to write, scenes to finish, a play to complete. Ironically, the better you follow this maxim to take time for discoveries, the more you are likely to accomplish and what you write probably will be more dynamic, honest, and inspired than if you rush.

A play isn't only people onstage talking to one another. It's a multi-layered, multi-dimensional kinetic construct of images, feelings, sounds other than words, characters' glances and gestures, the potential "meaning" in the setting and objects, the subliminal effects of color and accent, all happening in fluid "real" time. Be quiet and relaxed to sink into the layers of your play instead of skimming its surface. Describe each character and setting, each entrance and exit, in part because that helps you get into "the moment." Take time to awaken your sensory comprehension of a series of beats or an episode before you begin it. What does it smell like? Is it hot, cold, humid, foggy? What is the nature of the light? What sounds do your characters hear? Is anyone sleepy, or manic? Does the floor creak when they walk?

The characters will begin acting and reacting without coercion the more you engage all of yourself in the dramatic world. Don't bring your mind and your love of words alone—bring your senses and feelings fully. Observe and listen. Pay attention to what each character sees and hears in each moment so reactions will be honest and fresh. You might have a plan in your scenario for what each one *should* say, but as you embody characters without forcing anything you could discover exciting new possibilities. Don't artificially shut down a discovery. Look forward to writing each day so you can be surprised.

Perhaps your mind is too "busy" when you approach your work, jumping from idea to idea, leaping first to this character and then to that. Perhaps it's still buzzing from your active day. This "monkey mind" won't serve you. Playwright Sam Shepard, like novelist Jack Kerouac, says he lights a candle when he sits down to write. I have no idea why Shepard does that or what it means to him. This might be a lie. However, there is something quieting and ancient, even sacred, in lighting a candle, a reminder of less hurried times, of the simple light of inspiration. The slowly melting candle suggests a pace that serves imagination. A flickering light can be hypnotic; perhaps it relaxes the rational mind's hold on the creative self. This modest ritual sets "writing time" apart from the rest of the day and signals monkey mind to focus.

Great discoveries can spring forth when you're fully present. Other times small exchanges appear that might not push an action forward but are so entertaining that the audience really hears them. I suspect this entertaining beat in Tracy Letts's *Bug* was not planned:

> PETER.   It's a fucking bug.
> AGNES.   No, I know, what kind of bug?
> PETER.   An aphid, it's like a, a, a—
> AGNES.   A bedbug?
> PETER.   No, well, yeah, kind of, more like a louse.
> AGNES.   A louse? Like lice?
> PETER.   Not like head lice. They're more like plant
> lice.
> AGNES.   Like a termite.
> PETER.   No, that's more like a thrip.
> AGNES.   What's a thrip?
> PETER.   It's like a termite.
> AGNES.   Do you mean ticks?
> PETER.   No, a tick's like a flea, a thrip's like a termite.
> AGNES.   What's a bedbug like?
> PETER.   A bedbug.
> AGNES.   But what is a bedbug?
> PETER.   A bedbug.
> AGNES.   I thought it was just a nickname.

SUGGESTIONS FOR THE DAY:

1. Light a candle or create another ritual that reminds you to be still and present.
2. Read slowly through what you've written to be present and open to discovery.

Until tomorrow,
Linda

DAY 38

"When you're writing it's as if you're turning something over in your hands and making sure you're looking at every side of it. Is it a piece of coal? Or a lump of shit? But it could be a diamond! What's amazing about the creative process is how at each step you see so much that you hadn't before."

—**ROBERT CARLOCK**

STAGING YOUR IDEAS

Hi Writers,

Today I offer suggestions for how you can better embody your characters. Directors, designers and actors have to fulfill your ideas, but you should give them a play you can see and hear fully. Although your play might be adapted to various spaces, it begins with a very strong and specific vision that is entirely your own. Also, since plays are literature for reading, not just "blueprints" for production, do all you can to help a reader "see" what you see.

Why do I emphasize the value of making your theatrical world as physically "real" as possible? Until the middle of the twentieth century most playwrights had intimate knowledge of the theatre where their plays would be performed. Many had been actors and/or known most of the actors who would perform their work. The Greek playwrights knew every inch of the Theatre of Dionysus. In the early years playwrights were the protagonists and throughout the 5th century BC they were the director/ producers. Shakespeare was an actor in his plays as well as a producer and primary shareholder in both the acting company and the theatre house where most of the plays would be performed. So it was with Moliere in Paris. Today many writers create for specific theatre companies and stages.

Find a space the size of your stage. If you don't have enough space indoors, go outside. Walk the perimeter of the stage. Pace across and through it to get a feeling for the area your characters have to cover. Imagine the set pieces; walk around them. Imagine characters in beats or scenes you've written—how close are they to each other? How far are they from entrances? Consider the time it takes for a character to cross a room. When you next begin to write, this experience might inform the visual life of your play.

Create a tabletop model of your stage. Use small items like salt shakers, chess pieces or tiny action figures to "stand in" for set pieces and characters. Or, you might create what goes onstage out of cardboard. Position the people and setting the way you "see" them at the beginning of a scene and move them through the scene with your dialogue.

Are you paying attention to what's happening with all the characters onstage when only two are speaking to one another? Are you considering the theatrical effects of entrances and exits? If a character exits stage right—how realistic is it that the same character enters stage left within seconds? Do you imagine changes of settings? If so, be realistic about the time that takes and the effect the lack of action will have on an audience. Might you design for a scene going in the foreground, perhaps in front of a screen or curtain, while the set changes? Do you require costume changes between scenes? Take into account the time for that. Study the practicalities of stagecraft so you can know what is possible. You can buy apps such as Stage Write Software for planning staging.

The picture of the Theatre of Dionysus in Athens [p. 289] is of me looking onto it from the Acropolis. Behind and to my right is the Parthenon, the temple of Athena. This is the 2nd century BC version of the first Western theatre. In the 5th century BC the orchestra was a full stone circle. Nothing else was stone. Audience members sat on the hillside, probably on rugs they laid out the way we do for picnics. The first ring of seats might have been wooden ones for the Priest of Dionysus and visiting dignitaries. We think actors performed on a long wooden platform (sawhorse and trestle-style) just beyond the orchestra. Behind them was a wooden or skin scene house/tent of some kind ("skene" means "skin")— there probably was only one opening into the skene. Actors changed masks and costumes inside or behind the "skene." We speculate that choruses coming from town entered audience left because the town itself was in that direction. Those coming from the countryside came from the direction of the actual countryside, audience right. (Dionysus and his chorus might have entered audience left, the route from Eleusis, the god's birthplace.) The grove and temple of Dionysus are behind the stage; beyond them stretched forested countryside and mountains. Reading the plays, you can envision staging with this in mind. This is the foundation for much of Western drama.

SUGGESTIONS FOR THE DAY:

1. Find or create a space the size of your imaginary one.
2. Create a tabletop model of your stage with small items standing for characters. Study characters in action, paying attention to entrances and exits.
3. Draw, cut out pictures from magazines, papers, and/or copy from the internet anything that might belong in the world of your story and characters. This can help you create a visual understanding of images that belong in your dramatic world

Until tomorrow,
Linda

DAY 39

"A word is dead
When it is said,
Some say.
I say it just
Begins to live
that day."

—EMILY DICKINSON

SPEAKING FROM NECESSITY

Hi Writers,

In musical theatre, characters sing from necessity; their feelings are so strong they must burst into song. In plays, characters *speak* from necessity. They say only what they must in the moment. If you want a character to say something in particular, set up the circumstances for that to be an appropriate expression by that character in that moment. Save important ideas and revelations for moments when you should have the audience's full attention and when those spoken words will have the greatest impact. To claim that attention, usually something startling happens or is said, perhaps through a theatrical entrance or exit, or with the introduction of a surprising plot point. An angel crashing through a ceiling focuses an audience, and so does a sudden silence.

Speech is action. A character speaks to accomplish something—to flirt, plead, misdirect, persuade, invent an alibi, impress, and so on. Others listen with purpose—to learn, plan a rebuttal, buy time, seduce, discomfit. Know the action for each character at each moment. It's true that some characters babble or speak out of nervousness, while others pontificate at length, but even that falls under the rule of "must" since it is in the character's nature and is part of the dramatist's design. For instance, Winnie's prattle in Samuel Beckett's *Happy Days* is carefully constructed to illuminate ways in which some language serves to fill time, to give life the appearance of meaning. Winnie is driven to speak, though she says nothing of consequence.

In the Beginning have your characters say only enough to pique interest. Tease them with what might be ahead. Tony Kushner introduces the complexity and personality of Roy Cohn the first time we see him in *Angels in America*: "Roy conducts business with great energy, impatience and sensual abandon: gesticulating, shouting, cajoling, crooning, playing the phone, receiver and hold button with virtuosity and love." However, Kushner doesn't reveal Roy's goal. Necessity dictates everything Katurian says in the opening interrogation scene in *The Pillowman*. He struggles for his own and his brother's lives, trying to satisfy his questioners, never knowing what answers his captors want to hear. Katurian tells stories when he suspects those might spare him. He attempts to explain himself, argues, or retreats into submission. For Katurian speech and stories are survival tactics. Tragically, they both save and destroy him.

When characters find it easy to unload their deepest thoughts and fears as soon as the play begins, there's a danger that they have nowhere else to go, no secrets to hold for later revelations. What prompts them to speak, whether briefly or for long? Something someone else said? Perhaps something they read or heard before a scene begins? Why say what they must to this person? Why now? Are there people in the room who shouldn't hear what they have to say? Why *must* a character launch into a monologue? It's possible that everything a character says is a lie. Why must the character lie? Why now? Why this lie? Resist having a character say anything until it's clear why and what must be said, how that is consistent with the character, and how it furthers (or ends) the scene. Then, write all you think should be said.

Once the action moves past the set up and into the Middle, characters typically open up more, revealing themselves and additional vital information (usually through arguments or as punctuations to scenes). For dramatic effect have characters restrain full expressions of feeling until finally they boil over to generate crisis. Chekhov's characters often reveal a great deal about themselves when we first encounter them, but they go on to reveal even more subsequently to take us deeper and deeper into their hopes and misery. The early revelations are necessary for going the distance; they are only the beginning, not the peak, of the drama.

Characters can burst into song in a drama. It happens all the time in real life. You can illustrate friendships and family rituals this way. A song can menace, tease, flatter, embarrass, seduce, bond—any action you need. Apply the principles of having a song spring out of necessity and occur in a theatrically strategic place. Songs in *Language of the Body* and *The Tooth of Crime* comment on the action, expand themes, enable transitions in mood and action, and take us into inner thoughts. Musician KJ's opening song in Annie Baker's *The Aliens* sets up style, theme and expectations for the audience:

> TIME MACHINES WERE MADE FOR ME
> I BELIEVE
> IMPOSSIBILITIES
> ARE WHAT YOU PERCEIVE

SUGGESTIONS FOR THE DAY:

1. Review what you've written or planned so far with necessity in mind.
2. Is there anything your main character absolutely must say to one or more other characters? Write that now. Save it, though, for when it seems it must be said.
3. Who, how, when, why might songs be appropriate in your play?

Until tomorrow,
Linda

DAY 40

*"Writing a first draft is very much like watching a
Polaroid develop."*

—**Anne Lamott**

PLAYING WITH SIMILES ABOUT PLAYS

Hi Writers,

"Wrighting" a play is wresting a creation into being physically like a boat-wright, like shaping the staves of a barrel. The term comes from medieval English by way of Shakespeare and his contemporaries. Before their productions English folk saw theatre at festivals when short plays on religious topics were performed outdoors. Each play was produced by a local craft guild. Few people were literate. The literate person or persons who fashioned those plays were word "wrights," craftsmen like the others.

Consider creating plays as physical acts. Forget literary terms. How is playwrighting like painting? You select details of language and behavior to show (not tell!) actions that evoke recognition in the auditor. The auditor determines meaning for her/himself, but you guide it. How can paint on a flat surface awaken in us recognition of "truth" about "reality"? Plays may be like pointillist or impressionist paintings—daubs of color carefully arranged to give the semblance of what the eye has "known," leading the auditor to reflect on the scene as if s/he had never fully seen it before. Or, like the Mona Lisa a play presents an enigmatic subject with a background that evokes the mystical terrain of the soul.

Which is Chekhov's *Uncle Vanya* more like, plate juggling, a pot set to boil, a symphony? To me, it isn't like dominoes that fall upon one another in a chain the instant you push the first one, nor does it have the constant battling tensions of a basketball game. Horton Foote's plays seem like reservoirs filling with water, rising to the rim of the dam, and not like roller coasters. In *Vernon Early* the water breaches the dam at the very end. Perhaps *Waiting for Godot* has something in common with a song or symphony because of its choral repetitions, bridges, and thematic variations.

SUGGESTIONS FOR THE DAY:

1. Finding a good image for your play's action can help you construct the scenario.
2. How is playwrighting like plate juggling, basketball, a pot set to boil, a roller coaster, dominoes, a song, a dream, a symphony?
3. Can you imagine other comparisons for playwriting? Can you match those to plays?

Until tomorrow,
Linda

DAY 41

"What isn't said is as important as what is said."
—COLSON WHITEHEAD

THE SOUNDS OF SILENCE

Hi Writers,

Silence is a powerful dramatic technique. The audience will listen for what comes next—an effective technique for setting up main ideas. Silence can provide a rest for characters and audience to ruminate over what has just happened or been said. If something shocking is said or done, that space without words absorbs the impact. Writer Sally Nemeth explains the importance of silence in *Holy Days*: "If the director allows the characters . . . (after the opening exchanges) to sit and eat for at least a minute or two . . . it sets the audience up immediately to slow down and watch for the small stuff. Because so much happens in the 'small' stuff."

Perhaps a character uses silence to gather his/her thoughts and summon courage. The audience and other characters wonder what s/he's thinking. One character can refuse to answer another—out of fear, pain, anger, disgust . . . We watch in the tense silence and fill it in with our own feelings and questions. Deliberately taking time to speak, especially to respond to an attack (verbal or physical), is a character's way of exercising control. Characters might be engaged in a passive-aggressive relationship, each playing with silence to manipulate the other.

Characters might be waiting for someone to break the silence. This allows the audience to think about each character, what they might say, what they have at stake, which direction the next words could take the story. This is an especially potent technique when the audience suspects what is about to be said will have terrible or wonderful consequences. Imagine characters that have opened their hearts to one another. Afterwards they sit together in silence, needing no more words. Perhaps one reaches for the other's hand. A simple gesture can be more potent if it comes after a moment in which nothing is said.

Harold Pinter uses "pause" at times and "silence" in other instances in *Old Times*. Consider the difference between pausing and bringing the stage into complete silence. *Old Times* concludes with a long silent sequence of simple images of the characters, echoing the beginning and inviting the audience to recall all that has transpired. Vladimir and Estragon "wait" for Godot, their efforts to generate meaning for themselves punctuated by silences empty of meaning; the audience either fills those silences with their own questions and meanings or waits for the pair's next gambit.

Structurally silences can signal the ends of units of beats, a shift from one topic to another. Often silence punctuates the end of a scene or act— leaving the audience with a visual image and an emotional response to carry over a break in action or even through an intermission. A sound might break the silence—let that carry meaning or at the very least break tension.

SUGGESTIONS FOR THE DAY:

Are you using silence as a dramatic tactic? Who, how, when, why?

Until tomorrow,
Linda

DAY 42

"Writing and rewriting are a constant search for what you are trying to say."

—JOHN UPDIKE

SEARCHING

Hi Writers,

A first or early draft is never the final word. The search for satisfactory form and expression finds you at one moment spilling out dialogue, beats, and scenes, then doubling back on what you've written to probe for what you'll keep, what new questions you've raised. Next week you'll complete your set up and give more thought to the scenario for the Middle. Now is a good time to review everything you've written and planned for the Beginning.

Should you rewrite as you draft? The general principle is that you shouldn't do anything big to change your play now unless it truly is absolutely necessary, because you won't know until the End what you've created. You might see the need for an additional beat or two. If they come to you quickly without interrupting the flow of your writing, insert them. Otherwise, note in the margin a need for extra beats and don't stop to create them.

If you see something that probably will need major attention, note in the margin of your printed script and in your play journal what you question about that beat. There's a difference between rewriting and editing. You can cut or add in small ways as you work but don't stop your progress by doing huge revisions or cutting and shifting scenes around unless you're absolutely certain that should happen before you go on. Often that's your mind playing tricks on you. Finishing the draft should be your first priority.

If you decide to cut something you've written, run a line through it on hard copy and save it elsewhere, in case you change your mind. When you prepare for a full rewrite after you finish this draft you might wish you could remember that lovely monologue you wrote for the Beginning and then deleted.

If you are writing as if possessed and don't want to stop to review, gallop apace.

SUGGESTIONS FOR THE DAY:

1. Review characters, relationships, and plot logic—is anything changing? If so, how will that affect the rest of the scenario?
2. Fill out descriptions of setting, characters, entrances, exits and so forth that you might have rushed through while creating dialogue. Be sure you're seeing the play clearly.
3. What are you learning about yourself and your writing process?

Until tomorrow,
Linda

WEEK 6: THOUGHTS AND REMINDERS

- Decisions are at the heart of drama, reaction and change. Characters should make them onstage so the audience shares their thoughts and feelings.

- Know your inciting incident and why you've placed it where you have.

- If your inciting incident is early in the Beginning, conclude the Beginning section with a dramatic intrusion/hook that further focuses the action.

- Take time when you write to sink into the layers of your play and experience it with your characters "in the moment."

- Find a way to know your stage space physically.

- Create a model of your setting and move icons representing your characters in it so you can understand stage timing and the relationships of the characters to the space.

- Characters speak from necessity—theirs, due to action/reaction.

- Don't hesitate to let your characters sing—if it's necessary for them to do so and appropriate to the style.

- Playwrights wright plays.

- Playwriting is like—think of the shape of your action physically and visually.

- Don't be afraid to give your characters nothing to say. Use silence for effect.

- Review the Beginning and fully write directions and descriptions.

- Review, tweak, and edit earlier writing but don't stop to do large revisions—keep moving through the first draft.

- Observe new ideas for characters, theme(s), plot, theatricality and other aspects of your play before you begin the Middle section.

- Remember that as you write you are searching for what you want to say, so be not dismayed if it eludes you.

WEEK 7

TWISTING TO THE MIDDLE

You learn to think of your play as a musical composition while you create the transition from Beginning into Middle and design the scenario for the Middle. You pay attention to plot twists as they relate to character choices and inevitability. You are playing with language, making it active, concrete and visceral. You use narrative to clarify the play's spine.

DAY 43

"What is theater? It's an odd old-fashioned art form that places people who make believe in front of people who are willing to believe. It's also a sort of music, . . . you pay for a seat in a room with an orchestra and harmonies and overtones."

— ROB ACKERMAN

WHEN STRUCTURE IS MUSIC TO YOUR EARS

Hi Writers,

Hear the music of your play. A play is a musical composition with theme and variations, "harmonies and overtones," with a consistent ethos and focus. Usually a play has a "bridge" near the end that is consistent with what precedes it but somehow refreshingly breaks the anticipated pattern. Then the composition builds towards a culmination and resolve of the principal components. Aspire to overall aesthetic consistency. Plays work musically to affect emotion and memory, to express character, to ignite audience imagination. This is true for any kind of dramatic structure and style. Characters attempt fine tuning, or they resist it. They try to bring one another into or throw each other out of tune. They are being forced into action that might achieve balance or might drive them further from equilibrium. Some remain stuck in dissonance. Their struggles take them sharp and flat, building to crescendo, diminishing into silence.

Beats, units, and scenes are like notes, phrases, and other musical sections rubbing against one another to induce desire for resolve, sometimes yielding beautiful harmonies, other times clashing in dissonance. The audience needs variations and yearns for resolution. Great chord endings do resolve and yet often keep at least one note dissonant. Other compositions end in a way that is musically satisfying and yet highly dissonant. Musical variations build (with rests, decrescendos, and diminutions—not necessarily a simple uphill build) and culminate in necessity for some sort of resolution. Reaching that point of necessity, that crisis, you end the Middle and face the End.

Helen Deltz, a one-act by John Clark Donahue, exemplifies musical structure combined with an unorthodox approach to storytelling, an unreliable narrator, no protagonist, and an ensemble. Actors are themselves, not quite characters, gathered on a porch of a summer night. They weave a story about Helen Deltz, a character they create by implicit mutual agreement. Slowly they throw out ideas for which direction their story that night should take, listening to one another while looking out into the audience as if gazing into the street. Voices call out—a flute here, a trombone there. First there is some discord, but once all are excited about fictional "Helen Deltz" they build together, becoming more agitated as the story becomes more fantastic. The language is lyrical, images are vivid (she wore wooden shoes with little Chinese houses painted on them, and when it rained the people would come out and drown and die). The pace increases, actors' commitment intensifies. Like jazz improvisation, they play variations on their themes to delight one another.

Midway, actors pull out costume pieces and masks that had been hidden behind their backs. They don them with an item here and there. That escalates until everyone dresses and transforms while the story reaches fantastic dimensions. When storytelling, costuming and masking peak, some performers stand—a few walk towards the audience. This is the crisis. Suddenly they stop when they achieve a climax to the intensity and the story's potential. Then someone denies the whole story ("No, it wasn't Helen Deltz I was thinking of"). Performers pull back and remove costumes unobtrusively, as if embarrassed at being caught. They retract statements and pretend the story they told never happened. At play's end the actors are as they were in the beginning, with only bits of costume visible—a feather, a satin sleeve—as evidence of what occurred. Theatricality, musicality, and unpredictability make *Helen Deltz* fascinating.

SUGGESTIONS FOR THE DAY:

1. Review each beat, unit and scene of your Beginning for its musicality—variations, builds, rests, peaks. How do they contrast with or complement each other?
2. Investigate how musicality might guide the scenario you devise for the Middle. Will the Middle begin in a way that contrasts with and yet builds on the musicality of the Beginning?

Until tomorrow,
Linda

HOMEWORK FOR THE WEEK

1. Finish the Beginning.

2. Review the Beginning for its musicality, theatricality, intrusions, consistencies, dissonance, silence.

3. Experiment with hooks for the transitions from the Beginning into the Middle.

4. Add to the scenario for the Middle and revise as needed.

5. Review past letters for exercises you haven't attempted.

DAY 44

"What is writing a novel like? 1. The beginning: A ride through a spring wood. 2. The middle: The Gobi Desert. 3. The end: A night with a lover . . ."

—EDITH WHARTON

THE GOBI DESERT

Hi Writers,

You are preparing to draft the Middle of the play. Writers wrestle with the Middle because there are many decisions to make and a musical arrangement to consider as action moves onward, while keeping the possible outcome of the drama open and unpredictable. Like the whole play, the Middle has a beginning, middle, and end. Each of those has its ups and downs, its builds to punctuation and twists. In the Middle we can gain more intimate knowledge of characters and witness a variety of their interactions. You have time for memories and songs. Humor is most welcome in the Middle of a serious play. The audience is hooked into the story, so midway you reveal new aspects of characters. All characters have their turns in the spotlight and their subplots emerge. That makes their participation in the climax at the end more interesting and gives your theme more substance.

The Middle allows theme(s) to expand and plots to thicken. For example, Theresa's scenes with porn producer Len in *Boy Gets Girl* thicken the play thematically but aren't central to the action. It might be possible to drop Ophelia from Hamlet's story in the Middle, but doing so would diminish his character and audience empathy. If you are braiding multiple plotlines, the supporting plotlines can come more to the fore in the Middle. In *Part One: Millenium Approaches* of *Angels in America*, Kushner expands the plot points involving closeted gay Mormon Joe, his miserable wife, and Joe's mother who arrives to try to understand her son. This expansion enriches the play's themes of abandonment, faith and telling truths.

Fefu and Her Friends splits into multiple spaces in the Middle. Maria

Irene Fornes sets her characters in Fefu's living room for the Beginning and then divides them into four small groupings in separate spaces in the home. The audience also divides in four and travels from one room to another to separately experience those more intimate small scenes in the Middle. Audience members all gather together for the End—again in Fefu's living room—this time with more knowledge about all the characters than the characters themselves have about one another.

A play's Middle ends when the action tightens and the characters face crisis at its highest peak of intensity, when things simply cannot get worse, or more confused, or more urgent. Typically the protagonist or group of characters must face making a wrenching decision, or are confronted with dire consequences due to the crisis that has emerged from actions and reactions in the Middle. The transition from that crisis into climax is the transition into the End.

In a cartooned story the protagonist might struggle in quicksand, get rescued and rest on the river bank, then walk into the lair of a monster. In a character-driven story the stakes are personal and emotional while consequences for the protagonist become increasingly dire. These principles apply to an ensemble drama or a collage of scenes. The accumulation of ideas, opinions, images and feelings achieves mass and a sense that the theatre experience (like a performance of *Helen Deltz*) can't go much further.

Imagine a river. You led us into it with your play's Beginning, the setup of the stylistic rules, the introduction of characters and incitement of the dramatic throughline. Now we must cross the river with your characters. They might not see dangers lurking below the surface and will encounter travails. We don't know how or even if they'll all make it safely to shore.

SUGGESTIONS FOR THE DAY:

1. Review your Beginning. Can any exposition or character information be moved into the Middle so the Beginning tightens and you have more to work with in the Middle?
2. Return to the plot points you earlier imagined for the Middle. What more have you generated? Try again the approach of putting each on a card or piece of paper to experiment with arrangements (Day 22). Use the tactic of dividing the Middle into smaller segments to create a musically and theatrically effective pattern.

3. Apply the Boal technique to the Middle. See your characters at key plot points, especially its conclusion. What changes? What do you have to do to make that happen?
4. Refer to your logline—do you need to revise it as you contemplate the end of the Beginning and the shape of the Middle?

Until tomorrow,
Linda

DAY 45

> *"Sometimes we resist the conflict in our story because it scares us or feels forbidden. Remember that the desire to write is connected to the desire to evolve."*
>
> —ALAN WATT

THE PLOT TWISTS

Hi Writers,

Midway in *The 90-Day Play*, you're at a turning point while forcing characters to face challenges. Be bold. Continue to be open to stream-of-consciousness as you consider characters' behavior. Delve into the themes you're exploring, searching for what you don't understand about them as much as what you do believe. Don't worry about whether you're writing too much or too little. Let characters clash and the plot points rip, surprising yourself as you go.

There is a *turning point* near the end of a story in which a protagonist, faced with crisis, has an epiphany (for the Greeks, "anagnorisis," or "recognition") and decides to change or reverse course with his/her life. The Greek term for a turning point is "peripeteia." It can apply to any plot twist that turns the story in another direction, but that crisis moment is the most dramatic one. Not all stories end with a protagonist reversal—and yours might not. However, turnings and twists are your primary tools for carrying an audience through the drama. Just as it seems one argument is winning, another holds sway. When it appears a character will make an important decision, another character reveals something that shifts the plot in a different direction. One character's decision forces another's reaction, and that leads to a turn in the increasingly intense conversation or danger. Conflicts force reactions and decisions. Those, in turn, unearth revelations about fears, secrets, memories, dangers, and so forth.

A play that isn't story-based relies on aesthetic twists to retain audience attention. Think again in musical terms by shifting sequences from one tone to another, from somber to sardonic or from sentimental to relentless. With each shift you twist audience expectation and command their attention to your theme(s).

In the Beginning your protagonist and/or antagonists make choices that could send the action in several directions. The moment when one or more characters make decisions that thrust the action in its inevitable direction is a significant turning point—first the inciting incident, other times the end of the Beginning, and yet other times an important twist in the Middle. Marlene in Sally Nemeth's *Mill Fire* must decide if she will take the mill's money in compensation for her husband's death and if she will attend the memorial the mill is holding; with either one, she risks placing money above her husband's honor and being somehow complicit in the tragedy; yet, she needs money and the memorial will honor other deaths as well.

In the Middle, what people say and do are not as open-ended as they are in the Beginning. Imagine forcing a river through a narrow canyon and over rapids—there's no going back and the journey is increasingly fraught with tension as the Middle progresses. Through the Middle characters make decisions they hope will lead to resolution or agreement, but instead they seem to create more havoc, more conflict. They might try gambits they hope will make them safe but instead render them more vulnerable. Or, even though your protagonist does little, the characters around him/her behave in ways that narrow his/her options.

Usually an event or argument at the end of the Middle forces the action to turn towards an inevitable climax and conclusion. Here the emphasis is on inevitability—there is no going back, no changing course after this crucial twist. In arranging your scenario for the Middle, decide what that turning point into the End probably will be so can you build the other actions leading up to it. As you write through the Middle, something else might emerge as a better twist; it helps, though, to have one in mind.

SUGGESTIONS FOR THE DAY:

1. How does your Beginning twist as it ends to force action into the Middle?
2. As you draft the scenario for the Middle, think in terms of twisting and turning the plot. What do the characters do or what is done to them that forces the turns?
3. Sketch the turning point that might be the end of the Middle, the twist into the End, the boiling point of the action that precipitates Crisis.
4. What are you learning, how are you evolving as you face these challenges and twists with your characters?

Until tomorrow,
Linda

DAY 46

"I believe a playwright is a poet disguised as an architect."
—JEFFREY HATCHER

SOME WORDS ABOUT WORDS

Hi Writers,

Theatre provides one of the few live experiences in which we can delight in language together with others. Plays are like poems and architecture in that language and composition are primary elements. Relish this opportunity to put your best language skills forward. Choose words as delightful, appropriate and interesting as possible. Use words that are easily heard and recognized, unless it's characteristic for someone to speak in an almost incomprehensible and pedantic manner. Although usually we encounter that character in comedy, it can be used to good effect in a serious drama to break tension (Polonius in *Hamlet*, for example).

Something should always be happening with words in your play—

something that activates the plot, intensifies the drama, deepens character, or perhaps provides a much needed break for humor and counterpoint. Use active verbs to give the audience the sense of forward motion. In this exchange from David Mamet's *American Buffalo* characters are differentiated, the exchange is energetic, and the beat ends with a humorous punch that moves the plot forward:

> TEACH: That's a fact. A fact stands by itself. And we
> must face the facts and act on them. You better wake up,
> Don, right now, or things are going to fall around your
> *head*, and you are going to turn around to find he's took
> the joint off by himself.
> DON: He would not do that.
> TEACH: He would. He is an animal.
> DON: He don't have the address.
> TEACH: He doesn't know it.
> DON: No.
> TEACH: Now, that is wise. Then let us go and take
> what's ours.

Dramatic language should stimulate the audience's imagination. Make it as sensory and detailed as possible. Visceral, concrete language helps evoke visceral response in an audience. Violet in *August: Osage County* says to her daughter Ivy about her ex-husband, "Barry was an asshole. And I warned you from the start, didn't I? First time you brought him over here in his ridiculous little electric car, with that stupid orange beard and that turban." This paints a picture of Barry, conveys Violet's character, and in a brief snippet tells us how miserable Violet must have made poor Barry. Among Violet's husband Beverly's last words are, "My last refuge, my books: simple pleasures, like finding wild onions by the side of a road, or requited love." A single sentence awakens imagination and memory: Books, wild onions, requited love. By play's end we learn what that "requited love" means—key to his suicide and the family's misery.

Changes in language can illustrate changes in characters and action. Bev flutters around the house in *Clybourne Park* while Russ reads as the play opens. Trying to bring him out of his shell, Bev engages him in wondering what to call residents of various world cities. Eventually he plays with her and then finds delight in saying, "Ulan Bator." There is a dramatic contrast between his language at the beginning and the way Russ speaks when he erupts in the climax.

SUGGESTIONS FOR THE DAY:

1. What language do you most enjoy—in novels, songs, plays?
2. Do you recall when you first really listened to words? What were they? Why do you think they appealed to you?
3. As you review previous writing, note places where you might improve the language. If you immediately imagine small changes you like, "tweak" the script. However, don't spend time pondering it now—save that for the rewrite.

Until tomorrow,
Linda

DAY 47

"When I write a play I put aside my love of the classics and classical rules and sit down to create something that will please a seated Spaniard for five hours."
—**LOPE DE VEGA** (paraphrase and translation)

PRINCIPLES, NOT FORMULAE

Hi Writers,

While general principles of dramatic composition guide the creation of a play, they should not choke original ideas or block delightful flights of fancy. Some rules for drama emerged from descriptions of effective craftsmanship by classical authors Aristotle (*The Poetics*) and Horace (*Ars Poetica*). Scholars in centuries following took their observations to be rules for writing. The French Academy imposed formulae on Renaissance drama. Racine flourished within the "regles." Shakespeare wouldn't have been allowed to produce his work in France.

You introduce conflict and problems early if not from the outset and action accumulates intensity as the plot twists. Keep the audience wondering "What's next?"—concerned about the consequences, the stakes, of the action. You modulate the musical shape of the play and don't resolve rhythms and themes before the end. But there are many ways to accomplish your goals with no "one size fits all." A house has a foundation, walls and a roof, along with ways in and out. You can create secret chambers or organize rooms around a courtyard with an alligator pit in the center. In fact, you can build your home in a cave and forget about the foundation and roof. An audience yearns for imagination and originality more than conformity.

August: Osage County, by Tracy Letts, breaks some formulaic conventions while obeying general principles of audience engagement and originality. The set is a rambling many-roomed house. Interlacing storylines feature conflicts and travails of an ensemble more than the drive of a protagonist. First the author introduces us to his creation with a Prologue delivered by patriarch Beverly. This Prologue hints at the drama. Act I begins with the news that Beverly has left home and ends with the news that he drowned, probably of suicide. During that act most of the family gathers to contend with Beverly's disappearance. What Beverly has done is the inciting incident, for it brings everyone together. While Act I has four distinct Scenes, Act II has no scene divisions. After Bev's burial, scenes flow from one place in the house to another with more characters arriving and clashing, employing extended simultaneous dialogue. Having used the Middle to reveal dilemmas, Act III returns us to the scene structure of Act I. Plotlines overlap as they build to reveals and resolutions. They reach a crisis not for one protagonist but for an entire family. Climax and resolution occur when secrets are out of the bag. No character reverses course. Change happens within the family as an entity.

SUGGESTIONS FOR THE DAY:

How is your play entertaining the attention and thought of your audience more than trying to fit everything into a formula? See if fresh ideas occur when you set aside dramatic "rules."

Until tomorrow,
Linda

DAY 48

"I'm always pretending that I'm sitting across from somebody. I'm telling them a story, and I don't want them to get up until it's finished."

—James Patterson

NARRATING THE MIDDLE

Hi Writers,

Write through the Middle in narrative as if you're telling a story in third person. Whether this is a conventional linear storyline or not, you're laying out a theatrical adventure that can be described. In the early part of the playwriting process your play benefits when you develop characters in a theatrical setting. By now you have discovered that characters surprise you when they talk and interact in the multi-dimensional world of "play." Now you're working through arguments and tactics characters will use to arrive at a crisis and then climax. You're arranging plot points so they build in intensity while varying musically.

Narrating can free you to focus on plot issues, where you have decisions to make and what might be the most dynamic construction. Even if you're content with your process, try narrative as an exercise. This technique requires you to focus on the spine of action. You can't veer off course for long into your philosophical ideas without making a listener impatient. Pay attention to where you shouldn't linger on your themes. When you return to writing in the many simultaneous layers of dramatic form the narrative will provide support. However, be open to discovery from your characters. They might resist the narrative and take you in other directions.

What if you, instead of Marsha Norman, had the idea for *'night Mother*, a "two-hander" (two character play) with a single set and continuous action (no scene breaks)? It begins with Jessie looking for Daddy's gun. Soon after that, when the audience has had time to adjust to the setting, characters and language, Jessie announces to Mama that she's going to shoot herself. As the playwright, you now have a full-length play to write with those two characters, no outside intrusions, no other rooms, no the-atrical tricks to play. You know your ending—Jessie shoots herself off-stage. How will you fill the time between the inciting incident ("I'm going to kill myself, Mama") and that gunshot at the end?

Mama will try to talk her out of it—but how many ways can she try and how long can that go on without boring the audience? Jessie needs to explain herself; that can't fill up the entire play and we might tire of hearing it unless it varies. What else would happen in that situation? Mama would bargain with her, perhaps—I'll do this or that if you promise not to kill yourself. Mama will blame herself (either for real or just a ploy to gain Jessie's sympathy). Mama will beg, she'll claim she needs Jessie (how Jessie handles that is part of the action). Mama's strategy is to stop Jessie and each tactic is a unit or scene of action taken to achieve that strategy. Jessie's strategy is to succeed; she uses tactics to thwart Mama. You arrange those tactics so they progress organically and build to the crisis and climax. Mama must become more and more desperate. Jessie won't be deterred. The final unit is Mama's acceptance.

The units in between the Beginning and that acceptance can be con-founding. Each of those units is comprised of smaller tactics, each of which is a beat. Here's the breakdown of the first unit's tactics: Mama thinks Jessie is joking, the gun's no good, the bullets are too old, I'll call your brother, this is crazy talk, I'll call the doctor, you'll miss, if you want quiet go to your room (I'll turn off the TV), you'll go to hell, you can't use that gun because it belongs to me, you can't kill yourself in my house, you have a birthday coming up. Finally that first unit (or scene) shifts as Mama realizes Jessie is serious.

Threading through these argumentative tactics are other elements that bind the play and elevate it into a theatrical and thematic success. Jessie has been preparing for this; she made lists, arranged for deliveries, purchased food and items. Jessie has seen to it that Mama will be taken care of and won't simply be left in the lurch. She even plans to kill herself in a locked bathroom so Mama won't be accused of murdering her.

If you narrate your play through tactical units and smaller tactics you might discover new dynamics that excite you. It's possible that you will uncover some ideas that don't excite you but that you think you should put in the play. Either remove those or find a way to make them exciting for you—we want imagination, play, not formulaic expectations.

SUGGESTIONS FOR THE DAY:

1. Narrate your play as if you're sitting across from somebody, telling them a story, and don't want them to get up until it's finished.
2. What are your characters' strategies?
3. What tactics are they using to achieve their strategies?
4. How are they succeeding or thwarting one another?

Until tomorrow,
Linda

DAY 49

"[Y]ou don't teach piano playing at lessons; you teach how to practice—the daily rite of discovery that is how learning really happens."

— **JEREMY DENK**

FOR THOSE DAYS WHEN THE MUSE TAKES A BREAK

Hi Writers,

You're well into the play now. Congratulations. Take stock of how much you have created. Tomorrow you will begin writing the Middle, which usually is one-third to one-half of the whole. For a full-length play this is roughly thirty to fifty pages.

The more printed pages you generate, the more likely you are to have difficulty remembering where Character A told Character B something vital or where you placed expositional information about the story before the Point of Attack. You know you want to work on some sections in a rewrite but perhaps you can't easily find those sections now.

Today's exercises help you review and track what you've written "at a glance" before you generate more pages and plot complications. This work can unlock the Muse. It focuses your mind on the play while freeing it from the imperative to create. At times that's all your busy internal worker needs to release new ideas. With practice, you will shape your ideas into a play.

SUGGESTIONS FOR THE DAY:

1. At the same place on each printed page (top or bottom, corner or middle, whatever works for you), note in pencil any or all of these that might help you:
   - Where we are if you have multiple settings, or which area of a single set is being used
   - Who's onstage: a character list
   - If a character enters or exits
   - What happens on that page in a few active terms: "Sally reveals prison time"
     - Or, as a variation, note onstage conflict: "Charlene and Deon clash about Gary"
   - Exposition: "Justin's first marriage"
   - Foreshadowing/teasing about what's to come: "I'll tell you later, when we're alone."
   - Notes to yourself regarding anything to return to in rewrite.
2. Revisit your scenario to refresh your subconscious grasp of your overall plan and see if you need to make changes before going forward.

Until tomorrow,
Linda

WEEK 7: THOUGHTS AND REMINDERS

- Hear the music of your play.

- Create variations in intensity, tone, rhythm, and pace as you would in a musical composition.

- The Middle of a drama is the most challenging section—keep the End in sight as you play in the Middle.

- In the Middle you can expand themes and character development while moving the action forward.

- The Middle also has a beginning, middle, and end; each of those consists of even smaller components and tactics.

- Plot turnings and twists are key ingredients in driving action through to the End.

- A play turns and twists from external factors but more importantly from character conflicts, revelations, reactions, and decisions.

- It's not just *what* your characters say that counts—it's *how* they speak.

- Use active, concrete, visceral language.

- Adhere to flexible general principles for dramatic structure but don't let formulae choke your imagination.

- Narrating your story now like an excited fiction writer might help you perceive and arrange the plot points in your scenario so you can make it across the Gobi Desert of the play's Middle.

- When you can't create you can work.

UNIT THREE

MOVING THROUGH THE MIDDLE

You will experiment triangulating with your audience through language as you continue writing through the Middle to reach the End. You will give attention to emerging themes and make more formal decisions for the crisis and transition into the End. You practice varying the musical ethos of each unit of the play.

WEEK 8

BEGINNING THE MIDDLE— COLLISIONS AND THEMES

You will give more careful consideration to the words characters choose and their selection of comparisons to communicate with others. You will increase challenges, urgency and tensions for characters as you find ways to move the Middle forward.

DAY 50

KEN: Red is heartbeat. Red is passion. Red wine. Red roses. Red lipstick. Beets.
ROTHKO: Arterial blood.

—JOHN LOGAN, *Red*

TRIANGULATION: WORDS

Hi Writers,

When you read the words above, do you see "red"? Do you see, hear, smell, taste, reach into memory? The audience doesn't merely watch and listen—we recall with our senses wine, roses, arteries. Instead of using the color red to blush a subject's cheeks, Rothko made red a vibrant character. His painting invites you into your own private associations with the color. With language, as with visual theatrical elements, a play creates a *"triangulation"* effect by throwing a word or phrase into imagination and memory. The auditor reaches into that dimension to grasp the word and participate in "making belief." Think of a triangle formed by this, a meeting point in human experience that has no palpable form. The playwright creates a brainstorm.

Using words and phrases that operate like "red" is a technique you use carefully to heighten perception, to catch the audience's attention for important ideas and significant interactions. Use it as part of your play's "music," letting it rise like a crescendo out of rests and linear exchanges. Use this at times when the plot twists as well as in monologues and dialogue in which characters reveal their selves. When you select vivid words and phrases, know that they require more time than ordinary speech for an audience to ingest.

Here are examples of concrete words and phrases that invite the audience to triangulate:

- Shakespeare, *Macbeth*: "Is this a dagger that I see before me?"
- Harper, *Angels in America*: "there will be terrible rains and showers of poison light."
- Sarah, *Spinning into Butter*, Rebecca Gilman: "He's a poor crazy man. You'll always just stare at him on the train."
- Camae speaking of Martin Luther King, *The Mountaintop*, Katori Hall: "The Prince of Peace. Shot. His blood stains the concrete outside Room 306."
- Jessie, *'night, Mother*: "I found an old baby picture of me. And it was somebody else, not me. It was somebody pink and fat who never heard of sick or lonely, somebody who cried and got fed, and reached up and got held and kicked but didn't hurt anybody, and slept whenever she wanted to, just by closing her eyes."

SUGGESTIONS FOR THE DAY:

1. Which character or characters in your play uses language that triangulates? How?
2. Can you differentiate among your characters by the ways they use language?

Until tomorrow,
Linda

HOMEWORK FOR THE WEEK

1. Write the beginning of the Middle.

2. Practice language play, using exercises at the back of the book as needed.

3. Continue collecting in stream-of-consciousness.

4. Permit yourself to write out of scenario sequence if it helps you solve the Middle.

> 5. Identify theme(s) emerging as well as the theme(s) you began
> with. How might they complicate the action in surprising
> and suspenseful ways? How might they add to audience
> identification and empathy so that the play accrues more
> "meaning"?

DAY 51

*"I believe that the world is constructed of words and that
words have tremendous power and effect."*

—TONY KUSHNER

TRIANGULATION WITH COMPARISONS

Hi Writers,

Observe how the words you choose "triangulate" with your audience
through the most commonly used *figurative language*: the *simile*. A simile
is a direct comparison or likeness that uses words such as "like" or "as" to
relate two different things: Working for her is like—fill in the blank: walking barefoot through a pig pen, being waterboarded, getting stuck in traffic.
"My love is like a red, red rose." We use comparison to find something in
common with one another to connect us through triangulation. Nothing
is exactly like anything else and yet we use comparisons to share our lives.

What comparisons will your audience likely recognize? Contemporary people know a great deal through media, although the "hands on"
knowledge we share might be limited. I don't bee-keep or ski, but I can
imagine them. The Greek playwrights used comparisons for which their
audiences had visceral knowledge. They created drama for men they'd
gone to war with, men with whom they had crossed the Aegean and
hunted in forested mountains. Throughout their plays, therefore, war,
sailing (rowing), and hunting are the most commonly cited activities for
their similes.

Similes should be appropriate to your characters and their shared references. If Character A enjoys similes she will have to select references other characters understand (unless it's part of your plan that she's always saying things that baffle people). Use similes selectively. Too many jammed up together can overload an audience and diminish their impact. There are exceptions to that principle: Characters might hurl them back and forth in argument, as a contest, as compliments or as insults. If they are vivid, unpredictable and consistent with your theme(s), style and dramatic world, similes can enliven audience imagination:

- Mama in *'night, Mother*, referring to Jessie's and Daddy's epileptic fits: "Oh, that was some swell time, sitting here with the two of you turning on and off like lightbulbs some nights."
- Sarah in *Spinning into Butter*: "[I]t was like I had a viral infection that would flare up at the worst possible moments, and I started saying these . . . things."

SUGGESTIONS FOR THE DAY:

1. Which characters use similes? In what way?
2. Where are the moments where a vivid simile might be a useful tactic to catch audience imagination for an idea you're about to introduce? How does it function?
3. Might your characters share similes in dialogue? Who, when, why?

Until tomorrow,
Linda

DAY 52

"Tomorrow may be hell, but today was a good writing
day, and on the good writing days nothing else matters."
—NEIL GAIMAN

WRITER'S BLOCK DOESN'T HAVE TO BE AN OBSTACLE

Hi Writers,

You're excited, ready to work. You sit down (or stand), pen (or computer) in hand—and can't do anything. How can that be? You know the scene you're ready to write, you're enthusiastic. You've given yourself a transition into writing time. You lit a candle. Nothing comes to mind. Or, everything that appears in your imagination is boring; you reject it out of hand. Often something is stuck in your head, demanding to get onto the page and not letting any other ideas come to the surface.

What's commonly referred to as *"writer's block"* has many reasons for happening. Don't turn on yourself—this occurs to every writer. Focus on the work. Don't think there's something wrong with you, don't berate yourself and lose confidence. You can do this. Trust that your inner worker is telling you that today you need to work on something other than what you had planned. Be like water. Don't crash against the obstacle in front of you—find a way around it. More often than not, your subconscious needs to work more on your ideas for the play. It isn't quite ready for the scene you thought you would write today. Usually the problem is that you need to resolve aspects of plot, scenario, and/or character. Write in stream-of-consciousness. Even if everything you write today ends up in the trash, you'll clear your head and make way for the material you want to keep. Often, though, you'll discover that simply by writing whatever comes to mind you unleash exciting ideas you would not have accessed otherwise.

SUGGESTIONS FOR THE DAY:

1. Read aloud what you've written so far. Hearing the play can loosen new ideas.
2. Study the last material you wrote. Does something more need to happen—more beats, even another scene—before you continue? Is there a glitch in plot logic?
3. Study your scenario. It may well be that the scene you plan to write today doesn't belong here. The play might demand another series of beats, a whole unit, or possibly a new or different scene. Be open to revision of your plan.
4. What was happening musically in the section you just wrote? Perhaps you need a largo movement instead of the allegro you had planned for today. Listen to your play.
5. Meditating on theme allows insight into character and plot, and vice versa.
6. Research background information for the play. By focusing on facts you relax insistence on inventing something new, which often in turn sets free "the inner worker."
7. Go for a walk while you puzzle over what comes next. Laugh with friends, swim, fly a kite.
8. Envision moments and scenes out of sequence. Envision the crisis and the conclusion.

Until tomorrow,
Linda

DAY 53

"An idea, like a ghost, must be spoken to a little before it will explain itself."

—CHARLES DICKENS

THEME AND SPINE IN THE MIDDLE

Hi Writers,

Theme, characters, and spine are integrally related; theme is the marrow in the play's bones. Themes and viewpoints rise to a peak as action proceeds through the Middle. Revisit theme(s) you identified earlier. Are they shifting as you write, as you speak to your idea as Dickens says? Have new themes emerged? The theme(s), the big ideas that inspire you will help you discover the shape of the Middle the deeper you probe them, the more sides of them you examine and question. Argue with yourself, argue with your protagonist and antagonists; examine the opposite side of your own perceptions of your concept.

As you work through the Middle, consider how your theme(s) can become like characters, almost palpable onstage. The accumulation of thematic importance can be a technique for forwarding action and building towards crisis. Anton Chekov immediately sets up a problem with thematic implications in the inciting incident of *The Cherry Orchard*: An estate containing an orchard must be sold at auction to pay debts because feckless aristocrats can't manage it anymore. The aristocrats have no concept of making or saving money. Merchant (and former peasant on the estate) Lopahin tries to persuade them to sell the land and cut down the orchard for vacation rentals so they can keep the house and have an annual income. If they don't, the whole estate will be sold.

The delusional aristocratic diva won't listen to Lopahin, persisting in the fantasy that they'll be rescued without having to make decisions. Their conflict frames the action of the Middle. Its structure is more vertical than linear as the composition surprises us with theatrics, silliness, memories, and yearnings. Themes of loss of land, collapse of anemic aristocracy, rise of money-focused merchants, missed opportunities, human frailty, and

the consequences of disloyalty all rise up through the characters' interactions and speech. Lopahin stops trying to help the diva. Themes have
grown like the swell of a symphony's motifs as they approach crisis.

SUGGESTIONS FOR THE DAY:

1. Listen to your theme(s). How do they relate to the active spine?
2. Argue for and against every aspect of your theme(s).
3. How do your characters manifest themes? Where?

Until tomorrow,
Linda

DAY 54

"I placed a jar in Tennessee,
And round it was, upon a hill.
It made the slovenly wilderness
Surround that hill."
—WALLACE STEVENS

PLOTTING THE MIDDLE

Hi Writers,

The wilderness generated by your fertile imagination partners with form
to create a work of art that can't exist without both. To help you fashion
formal decisions, I will review this month structural aspects of various
plays—concentrating on the Middles. We'll examine how writers have
composed forces in dynamic interaction—opposition, incongruences,
dissonance. We'll listen to the music of plays. I'll analyze how plays modulate the action of the Middle, breaking units of rising tension with scenes
of character and theme revelation. Rarely does the tension climb steadily
beat by beat. Like a symphony, a successful play uses rests as well as soft
and slow movements for thematic depth and to prepare the audience for

another climb in intensity. And we'll see how theme and character blossom in the Middle.

Set in a modest home, the action of *'night, Mother* is continuous. Early in the play Jessie announces to Mama without histrionics that she's going to kill herself. We learn through the course of the play what in Jessie's life has led to this moment. The writer saves the most intimate and searing personal information for the Middle and climax. Norman doles out Jessie's story slowly, piquing our curiosity. When Jessie announces her plan, Mama's first reaction is disbelief. A series of beats comprise a unit we might label "Denial." Jessie has a calm and rational answer for every tactic Mama uses to dissuade her. Mama realizes Jessie really means it. That provides transition into the next unit of beats. In this Mama questions (What's this about? How long have you been thinking of this?), and also tries bargaining (We can fix it). Call this unit "Questioning and Bargaining." Mama erupts in "Anger" in a short unit of beats: "It's your own sweet fault," and "I can't do anything," Jessie has decided. Note that this is a short unit—musically it punctuates the longer two preceding it by being intense and yet variant.

After Denial, Questioning and Bargaining, and Anger—with their musical differences and hints at Jessie's life story—we move into a "Truce." Mama buys time. She makes cocoa and offers for Jessie to talk about something else. The audience doesn't need for the action to drive ahead at this time, possibly because we, like Mama, want Jessie to change her mind. That Truce doesn't last long. As Jessie probes about Daddy and another woman, Mama erupts once more in "Anger." She becomes irrational and self-centered, which increases tension and turns up both volume and pace musically. We understand why Jessie doesn't want to live with Mama.

Mama moves the play into a short unit of beats that combine Denial and Anger as she gets Jessie to talk about her ex-husband. One moment Mama is saying he didn't love Jessie, the next moment she suggests Cecil might be ready to reunite. Several tactics merge here and Mama is losing control. The intensity level of the play climbs with her antics. In this part of the Middle you, like Norman, can let many factors collide in what might be a "false crisis."

It's time now for another break in the tension. The audience can listen to more about Jessie. Mama has one more Bargain: Daddy had fits, too—Jessie can control them, they aren't enough to make her want to die.

We're ready at last to hear Mama describe Jessie's fits in vivid detail. The driving action has created anxiety and suspense. Mama moves in for her final pitch: You haven't had a fit for a year, your new medication is working. Yes, Jessie counters—Now that she can see her life clearly she knows she must end it. The play moves into crisis. Mama is out of arguments. She begs, bargains, tantrums, thinking mainly of herself—you're my child. No, I am what became of your child. With that, Jessie shuts her down and the play makes the transition from Middle into End.

SUGGESTIONS FOR THE DAY:

1. Identify the components of your Middle, the tactics used by the characters that drive as well as those who thwart, without worrying about the linear composition. Write each of these ideas on a separate note card or piece of paper (refer to directions for this in Day 22). Try to give each a title like "Denial" or "Bargaining."
2. Identify the character and thematic material that might be reserved for the plateaus in the rising intensity. You may discover you need to edit earlier sections where you revealed too much about characters in order to place that information, those stories, here where the audience is better primed to hear them. Again, place each of these character and theme ideas on a separate card.
3. Experiment with the arrangement of these ideas on a large surface, keeping in mind the goals of variations in tempo, musicality and tone as you build dramatic intensity. The plot points might follow a linear alignment (some call this a "clothesline") while theme and character ideas will build vertically or circle off that linear organization.

Until tomorrow,
Linda

DAY 55

"[T]he rough drafts of all true artists are a mess of deletions and corrections, marked up from top to bottom in a patchwork of cuts and insertions that are themselves re-crossed out and mangled."

—ANTON CHEKHOV

VERTICAL ACTION

Hi Writers,

Based more in character and atmosphere than a strong inciting incident, Anton Chekhov's *Uncle Vanya* builds vertically, like a symphony or a tone poem that accumulates layers and density of theme as it moves forward in time. We are thrust into the quotidian life of people on a provincial Russian estate. The main characters are on edge. Each character voices discontent, regrets, longings, and peevishness with others. They are appealing in their vulnerability, familiar in their desire to face mortality with more to show for their lives. We get the sense that something is about to happen, for these people seem at their breaking points.

This discontent increases in Act II, the beginning of the Middle, set at night. Characters with insomnia speak as if walking and talking in their sleep. Sonia, the Professor's daughter and Vanya's niece (Sonia's mother died), is the only character who works hard and cares for others without complaint. She chides both her uncle and the visiting doctor, Astroff, for turning to vodka to dull their existential pain. "When one has no real life, one lives in illusions," Vanya replies. The doctor reveals his attraction to Elena; however, he also declares he can't love anyone. Alone after Astroff leaves, Sonia spills out her love for him. Elena probably has fallen for Astroff, but she won't betray her marriage. Act II ends with these intimate confessions. Dissonance within characters propels the play forward.

As Act III begins (a continuation of the Middle) the Professor has asked everyone to assemble. Minutes before the meeting, Sonia reveals to Elena her deepest feelings for Astroff and her fears he can't love her because she isn't pretty. "I'll talk to him," Elena promises. The impending meeting and Elena's promise set in motion conflicts that will push characters into crisis, climax, and turning points. In one sense we might say the play only begins in Act III. However, without the vertical layering of characters and situations in the first two acts the audience would have no way of feeling empathy for these people. Instead of responding with sensitivity to the news that Sonia suffers from love for him, Astroff foolishly declares his love for Elena, who rebuffs him. As he tries to kiss her, Vanya enters with flowers for Elena (whom he also loves) and witnesses Astroff's attempt. Distraught, Elena begs outraged Vanya to use his influence so she and her husband can leave, today if possible. The dramatic pot is boiling. Let's call this "first crisis." A third crisis will end the Middle.

The Professor interrupts that collision of Astroff, Elena, and Vanya. The elderly egotist wants to sell the estate so he'll have money to live someplace more urban. The Professor has given no consideration to what will happen to people dependent on the estate. Vanya reminds the Professor that the estate has passed to Sonia since it had belonged to Sonia's deceased mother. Furthermore, Vanya sacrificed his inheritance (and his dreams) to pay off the estate's debts for his sister's sake. Vanya blows up—revealing his hatred for the Professor and his rage at what his life has become. He storms out. This is the "second crisis." We hear a shot, which sets up Vanya's entrance with a gun for the "third crisis." He shoots at the Professor—and misses: Climax. Vanya gives up; he's so incompetent he can't even kill a man. Elena pleads, "Take me away from here!" Act III—and the Middle—ends with this serio-comic misery and disruption. The final act (the End) concludes the fireworks of Act III with a slow decrescendo, allowing the consequences of the Middle to settle into the audience while all accept their fates.

The playwright builds a beautiful drama by taking us quickly into characters' deepest thoughts, fears, feelings, and dreams. *Uncle Vanya* achieves variety and momentum through clashes and calm, clashes and calm. Monologues and soliloquys pepper beats and units of dialogue. Distraught characters move on and offstage, often interrupting scenes, to provide a sense of forward movement and pique curiosity. The play achieves its urgency for resolution through characters out of balance that yearn for harmony they never can achieve.

SUGGESTIONS FOR THE DAY:

1. Can you take us deeper and deeper into your characters' inner lives as the play progresses, building in layers? How?
2. Study Chekhov's characters' monologues and soliloquys for dramatic writing that captures stream-of-consciousness and internal dissonance.

Until tomorrow,
Linda

DAY 56

"Whatever our theme in writing, it is old and tired. . . . It is only the vision that can be new, but that is enough."
—**EUDORA WELTY**

UNIVERSAL THEMES: HUBRIS AND HAMARTIA

Hi Writers,

Even the silliest comedy is "about" something thematically because you're illuminating human behavior from the ridiculous to the sublime. Several themes have occurred in one form or another over the twenty-five hundred years people have been writing plays. They're in old epics and contemporary novels as well. We wrestle with them and observe how others' battles with them affect our personal, social, and political lives. They might very well be in your play.

Hubris and *hamartia*. "Hubris" is a Greek concept you might have seen referred to as excessive pride. The word calls to mind the image of a river swollen over its banks to flood. When pride overwhelms a character beyond what is reasonable and civil it can cause great damage. The Greeks usually combined hubris with "hamartia," meaning: missing the mark. Think of an archer so out of balance that her aim is off or she shoots for the wrong goal. Together, pride swollen out of boundaries distorts vision, causing us to miss the mark or choose the wrong target. When we in the audience observe hubris in any character, we have the opportunity to reflect on how it works within ourselves as well as others in our lives.

Plays hold a mirror to nature so we might see ourselves more clearly and make better choices. A person might begin in balance, get puffed up by other characters' praise, commit hamartia by taking wrongful actions, and then fall in defeat. A character might begin in hubris and end deflated through either his/her inner awareness or from attacks by others. The hubristic character might never see the light while others suffer. Or, that person might finally achieve clear sight, bring pride into balance and achieve harmony in self and others. Moliere punctures Tartuffe, a pseudo-religious demagogue whose outsized self-importance ultimately blinds him to the possibility that someone might cut him down to size. The Music Man in the musical by that name enters River City believing he can flimflam people into buying trombones, take their money, and leave before they realize they've been scammed. Faced with innocence and honesty, though, he finds the ability to change and become his best self.

SUGGESTIONS FOR THE DAY:

1. Does any character in your play have hubris? Why? What can happen in your play to puncture that? Is a character clinging to unwarranted and excessive pride in a way that blinds him/her? If s/he could stop being so stubbornly proud, might that change the course of events or at least alter his/her relationships with others?

2. Does any character in your play aim for the wrong goal through hubris or perhaps another reason? How? Why? How does that affect the action?

Until tomorrow,
Linda

WEEK 8: THOUGHTS AND REMINDERS

- Triangulate with your audience through words and comparisons—make them active players in your game.

- Be like water—flow around obstacles.

- Continue stream-of-consciousness collecting and imagining through the writing process.

- Listen to your characters.

- Listen to your play.

- Continue exploring your themes.

- Increase challenges and urgency for characters through the Middle.

- Narrow the options for your characters through the Middle.

- The dynamic interactions of your play's Middle can be created through many means, including oppositions, incongruence, dissonance (internal and external to characters), arguments, and characters' shifting tactics.

- Dramatic tension rises, hovers on plateaus, then builds again as it aims for crisis at the end of the Middle.

*You can build a play with a vertical as well as a linear structure.

- Be alert for universal themes at work in your play—themes you might not have imagined when you began.

WEEK 9

COMPLICATIONS, TEXT AND SUBTEXT

Y ou will explore new approaches to characters' physical and vocal behavior, as well as themes of illusion, self-deception, and deceit. This week you will learn to score your play's musicality through key plot points. You will give consideration to the use of vivid language and metaphor, using the past for dramatic effect, and the nature of text and subtext.

DAY 57

"Somewhere, maybe, is a tongue with words for what we do, how it lands on the human spirit, how we share space and time, story, myth, intention, and feeling. Somewhere there's an idiom of our being together—a dialect of presence."

—TODD LONDON

UNIVERSAL THEMES: ILLUSION

Hi Writers,

Some people suspect that all we believe is an illusion, a fabric of concepts designed to help us navigate the mysteries of living. Do any of your characters address the illusions by which they live? Do they insist that others do? If their illusions are challenged, how do they respond? Or, do they believe there is a concrete "reality" separate from "illusion"? It isn't necessary to create people more complicated than folks next door to fashion characters whose illusions about self and life generate serious or comedic consequences. Examine your story, characters and plot for the possible role of "illusion."

Calderon de la Barca's *Vida es Sueno* addresses that theme in its broadest sense as well as its most individual. Translated as "Life is a Dream" (I prefer "Living is Dreaming"), the characters begin with solid social constructs about who they are, what their relationships are to one another, and how they should behave. They are not happy in those constructs; in fact, one is imprisoned and another must disguise her gender. As events test beliefs, the leading figures strip away constructs to perceive another sense of self and loyalty. Ultimately, the characters must decide which belief structures to follow based on what appears best for all.

The Spanish word for "illusion" is "engano." Besides illusions about life, it also means deceit, especially self-deception. Arthur Miller's salesman Willy Loman's life is falling apart because he clings to fantasies about himself and his sons and impresses those illusions on his family. Characters in Caryl Churchill's *Cloud 9* are locked in stereotypic gender, class, and ethnic roles in Act I. Set in British Colonial Africa, 1880, they show us in comic and tragic ways how these illusions mask secret behaviors and thoughts that are rotten at the core. These characters achieve liberation from those earlier illusions in Act II, one hundred years later. Perhaps they are engaging in new illusions, but in 1980 they are healthier and happier: "[I]f there isn't a right way to do things you have to invent one."

SUGGESTIONS FOR THE DAY:

1. Do any of your characters have to examine illusions? How and why?
2. Does more than one character face a crisis forcing recognition of those illusions? How? What are the consequences?
3. Can you build towards that crisis with tactics, tearing away the veil bit by bit?
4. Your main character's ultimate collision with illusion can form the final unit of beats in the Middle of the play and be the trigger for crisis. Examine that possibility.

Until tomorrow,
Linda

DAY 58

*"[B]eing creative is not summoning stuff ex nihilo. It's
work, plain and simple—adding something to some other
thing or transforming something. . . . There's always a
way to get something to do something to do something
else."*

—**MICHAEL ERARD**

AN ACTING TECHNIQUE:
WEIGHT, SPEED, LINE, ATTITUDE

Hi Writers,

Imagine characters in terms of *Weight, Speed, Line, and Attitude.* Imagining how characters might move and speak can give you new ideas for decision-making and emotional reactions as they approach crisis. Also, each character should be different from the others; use those differences for visual and musical variety. I was introduced to today's techniques in classes at the Dallas Theatre Center in 1968.You can read about the SITI Company's version of them in *The Viewpoints Book*, by Anne Bogart and Tina Landau.

Weight: A character might be heavy or light (or somewhere in between), regardless of body weight. Some overweight people are light on their feet, for example.

Speed: A character might move very quickly or slowly, briskly or with languor.

Line: A character could cross a room in a straight line or curve through space, staying close to the edges. Someone might characteristically stand up straight with "good" posture or slump. How do your characters hold themselves and what does that say about their sense of self?

Attitude: Which characters are timid? Which are bold? How do their attitudes towards themselves and others affect the play's action?

Apply this technique to *sound production*. Does one character speak softly and another bray? Does one take his time getting to the point while another is blunt? Does anyone try to command conversation with volume or speed?

Does Jessie stride quickly and boldly with straight posture in *'night, Mother*? What about the Professor in Uncle Vanya—does he have a light voice, slump, and walk hesitantly? You might think that all this is left to actors and directors in production. However, the production takes its cues from your creations.

SUGGESTIONS FOR THE DAY:

1. Practice this technique by observing people as well as characters in television and film.
2. Try the technique above as you imagine more facets of your characters.
3. Write a stream-of-consciousness monologue for each character using this technique—imagine their inner thoughts as they respond to a key plot moment in the Middle of the play. How do they stand or sit as they speak? What is their vocal behavior?
4. Do any of your characters change in the course of the play? How might their inner changes be manifest in external characteristics?

Until tomorrow,
Linda

DAY 59

"I often think in music. I live my daydreams in music. I see my life in terms of music."

—**ALBERT EINSTEIN**

SCORING THE ACTION

Hi Writers,

You can chart the action of your play like a musical score. Today I illustrate a macro version of this, selecting major plot points in *Uncle Vanya*, *The Cherry Orchard*, and *Clybourne Park*.

See the charts of plot points at the end of this letter.

My interpretations of the rising intensity of action and the placement of key events are rough, but you should be able to grasp the concept. You can see the shape of your play and listen to its "movements." Adapt this scoring concept to smaller units, scenes, and beats.

Uncle Vanya
1 – Vanya argues with Mother; 2 – Vanya declares love for Elena; 3 – Sonia fawns over Astroff; 4 – Sonia confides in Elena; 5 – Elena promises to talk to Astroff; 6 – Astroff tries to kiss Elena; 7 – Professor wants to sell/Vanya erupts; 8 – Vanya shoots and misses; *9 – Vanya tries to steal morphine; 10 – Vanya, Sonia and Mother face the future alone

The Cherry Orchard
1 – Estate to be sold; 2 – Lopahin's plan to keep house/Mama evades; 3 – Lopahin begs/answer me; 4 – Lopahin's last request; 5 – The estate was sold; 6 – Lopahin bought it; *7 – Lopahin doesn't propose to Varya; 8 – All but Fiers leave. Sound of trees being downed.

*In both plays Chekhov places an important moment in the conclusion that is less intense than the crisis or climax: Astroff prevents Vanya from committing suicide and Lopahin chooses not to propose to Varya. In each play, the moment adds spice to the End and closes a subplot. Although the action subsides in the conclusions of both plays, the emotional resolutions are powerful.

Observe the shapes of action in the two acts of *Clybourne Park*. What do the shapes of all the plays have in common and how do they differ? Inciting incidents don't always happen early and conclusions don't always taper off, for example. Both acts of *Clybourne Park* begin with no drama. Act I heats up as first Russ's 1) minister and then 2) bigoted neighbor, Lindner, pester him. It continues to build as people argue and we grasp the racial underpinnings of Lindner's antagonism. 3) That arguing alone could be a crisis. However, the 4) footlocker belonging to Russ and Bev's son who committed suicide in the house slides downstairs to bump the action even higher. 5) Russ erupts not just at Lindner's racism but as a wounded father defending his son. The climax comes as 6) he begins to read Kenneth's suicide note, taken from the footlocker. 7) Intensity slowly subsides while others leave Russ and Bev alone to try to restore order.

The second act begins in a new key. African-American Lena 1) tries to gain the attention of the white couple buying the house for what she has to say about the house and the integrity of its history. She's named for her aunt, the woman who purchased the house from Russ and Bev. 2) Once Lena finally asserts herself, the play erupts into 3) bickering that increasingly focuses on racism as white characters deny they are racist while behaving in stunningly racist ways. Then Lena and her husband 4) reveal the suicide in the house. When animosity among these people explodes into 5) crisis, a workman brings the 6) footlocker onstage and retrieves the letter. 7) Lights shift as we move to an even higher intensity that is emotional and thematic for climax. Kenneth descends the stairs in uniform. It's 1957. 8) He writes his suicide note while the actor who played Russ reads it aloud. Themes crescendo over story at the end.

SUGGESTIONS FOR THE DAY:

1. Chart your action as a musical score with the plot points you have drafted for your scenario. Use only the major points of conflict you have in mind, especially for the Beginning and Middle. You might find it helpful to use graph paper.
2. Score an important unit you've written, like the first segment of the Middle.

Until tomorrow,

Linda

DAY 59: Scoring the Action — Graphs

Bottom line = lowest intensity.

UNCLE VANYA

THE CHERRY ORCHARD

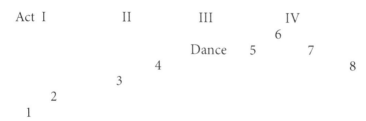

CLYBOURNE PARK

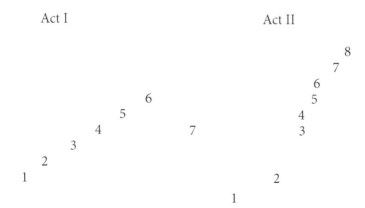

DAY 60

*"Pay particular attention to the myriad sensory responses
that precede and supersede the words that a person is
speaking. Especially in moments of self-revelation or
clarity about his destiny, pay attention to what the person
is listening to, where his eyes are looking, what his fingers
are touching. . . . [T]he words we speak are only a tiny
part . . . of our total response.*

—DAVID DOWNS

CHARACTERS IN THE MIDDLE

Hi Writers,

Whatever the form of your play, the audience is watching characters, listening to them, learning from them. In the Middle you build character conflicts or dissonance in stages so they reach the highest point of intensity at the end of the Middle—forcing resolution. The more facets of a character, the more engaged the audience is with the action rising through the Middle. Inhabit each character each moment as an actor might, regardless of your play's genre and style. Read your play aloud in the time it should take characters to speak. Listen to what another character says and don't think any further. Feel the reaction. Imagine the sensory experience. You will discover more original approaches to each beat.

What's the temperature in the room? What does it smell like? Is there an open window? What can they hear from outside? How are your characters dressed? Does a character need to shed a jacket or put on a coat? Does anyone need to buy time by massaging a foot? If the characters are outside, is there a breeze? Does it look like it might rain? What time of day is it? Are there clouds to watch? What scents are in the air? Is the character's temper taking hold of reason? Is his/her body heating up? Does s/he have control of what s/he's about to say? Did what the other character say or do activate an old memory, an old hurt? Is s/he hiding a secret?

Revisit what you've written to inhabit your characters and investigate sensory reactions and unspoken feelings. Often you will discover a scene beneath a written scene that moves a bit differently like a current below the surface of a river. When you explore that deep current you might find new beats and texture for what you poured out earlier. And those discoveries will fuel tomorrow's writing. They all fit together. If characters are only broadly outlined, add elements to make them more interesting: Your villain might have a phobia about shaking hands and a secret he hides, for instance. Trust that diving deeply into the characters will give you momentum and fresh ideas for how to lift the action more subtly.

SUGGESTIONS FOR THE DAY:

1. What makes your characters angry and how do they react when angry?
2. What can make them feel hurt or wounded, and how do they react to that?
3. What can others do to make them feel respected? How do they respond to that?
4. Do they fear anything they don't let others know about? How is that manifested?

Until tomorrow,
Linda

DAY 61

"[W]ith a few exceptions every word traced back far enough is either a metaphor or an onomatopoeia."
—JOHN CIARDI

TRIANGULATION: VIVID WORDS AND METAPHORS

Hi Writers,

You are creating an imagined world where language is selected and heightened. Whether you can create that world of words on the first draft or the tenth, it should be a goal. Give your characters language that can inspire your audience to be more alert to words. And don't neglect invent-ed words— from comedic play by Aristophanes to "supercalifragilistic-expialidocious," writers have the corner on this market. In this first draft place no restraints on your characters' ways with words. Choose words that evoke memories and wake us from the ordinary.

Poet Ciardi reminds us to consider how language began. Most verbs, nouns, and qualifiers had an association with their references that people could recognize and remember. The Greek "thalassa" is an onomatopoe-ic word meaning "the sea." It sounds like waves caressing a shore. Hear waves and see the image in the shortened version, "sea." A word that is "vivid" is alive with sounds, images, smells, and visceral experiences of life. Some early languages included mimicry of bird songs and the use of whistles. Sounds were made with the tongue and breath. A geographic place might be named for a birth or a battle; in that case a word sug-gests a story. Ancient humans also created words for the sheer joy of it, to make one another laugh and think. Some created alphabets with glyphs or ideograms that associate words with images. Ernest Fenellosa's essay "On the Chinese Written Character as a Medium for Poetry" inspired modern Western poets by urging a focus on the images words evoke.

A *metaphor* is a term used for one object that is transferred to an-other, different object; unlike similes, metaphors don't use "like" or "as." The evening of life. The winter of our discontent. The storm-tossed sea of love. The cream in my coffee. Metaphors help characters find com-parisons through which they can share feelings and observations. With metaphor, one character "triangulates" with others and with the audience as well. Klytaimestra [sic] (in Anne Carson's translation of *Agamemnon*) uses corny metaphors to shower false praise on the husband she plans to murder: "I salute my man: he is the watchdog of the palace, forestay of the ship, pillar of the roof, only son of his father, land appearing to sailors lost at sea, fine weather after storms, fresh stream to a thirsty traveler." The Chorus threatens to stone Aigisthos after he and Klytaimestra kill Agam-emnon in Aeschylus's play. Aigisthos replies: "Don't squawk at me from your seat on the lowest rowing bench: I run this ship. Know it."

SUGGESTIONS FOR THE DAY:

1. What metaphors might be consistent with your theme(s)?

2. Are any of your characters more likely than others to use metaphor? What, why, when?

Until tomorrow,
Linda

DAY 62

"We are most of us by nature secretive creatures. . . . In making characters reveal themselves they must be given a cause, a motive."

—ALAN AYCKBOURN

THE PAST IN THE PRESENT

Hi Writers,

It's the rare enlightened Buddha who doesn't carry the past with him or her in thoughts, stories, actions, reactions, desires, regrets, and self-image. Often we don't know how our pasts affect us until an event in the present brings us up against it and demands we recognize its influence. This is the stuff of drama—confronting what we avoid or what we didn't even know was influencing us. Characters usually conceal effects of the past as a play begins. Circumstances bring those feelings to a boil in the Middle. Feelings erupt and consequences either drive the action to another boil or resolve. References to the past both move the action and/or theme forward and help the play expand in the Middle to achieve vertical growth.

In the Beginning it might be necessary for the audience to know something about a character's past. Provide a glimpse of that past with the sense that there's a larger story yet to tell. This is part of how you move the play forward. A character might reveal something hidden as a dramatic intrusion that propels the action in the Middle. Otherwise, though, characters usually protect themselves from revealing much. Or, they simply don't understand the role the past is playing and will have to recognize that as the action proceeds. Oedipus' denial of his role in the past is the key action in that play; crisis demands his recognition.

Characters don't give up their pasts easily. Rothko's assistant Ken in *Red* refers briefly in Scene 2 to his parents' death. Rothko pushes Ken to talk about how colors make him feel. Ken says only that white reminds him of the snow outside the room where they died. In Scene 3 as the men paint a canvas red together, Ken responds emotionally: The red is like the dried blood on the carpet where his parents died. Rothko probes, "What happened . . .?" Ken resists, "I don't want to talk about it." Rothko urges Ken to "Go into all that white." Rothko's challenge leads Ken into the significance of his past and deepest emotions, and so on to independence.

Like Rothko, characters should pry. Why must anyone reveal anything to anyone else? What forces people to blurt out impulsively or in anger something they've held within? How can revealing the past help a character move into a new understanding? Not only do you create motives and tactics for these revelations, but you also give time for the chain of action/reaction that might follow. In Rob Ackerman's *Call Me Waldo*, Lee becomes possessed by the spirit of transcendentalist Ralph Waldo Emerson: The playwright teases our curiosity about why Lee is spouting lines from Emerson by slowly revealing he is trying to cope with emotions brought up by his daughter's recent near-death. If we knew that from the beginning we would lose the play's spine. We come into realization with Lee as he transcends his fears.

There's always the possibility that a character is lying about the past, coloring a memory, avoiding truth. Do other characters call it a lie? Do they force the truth into the open? If several characters share the same past experience, does each recall it differently? If so, consider the fireworks that discrepancy can spark. *Pillowman, Landscape of the Body* and *Old Times* offer fascinating examples of characters who spin tales about the past that may or may not be true.

SUGGESTIONS FOR THE DAY:

1. Review where and how characters have told about the past in what you've written so far.
2. Have they given away too much of the secrets and memories they hold within themselves? Can you reserve any revelations for later in the play

to greater effect?

3. Where might you place those revelations later in the scenario?
4. What revelations remain for later? Are you satisfied with how you're preparing for them?
5. How are reactions to revelations moving the play forward?

Until tomorrow,
Linda

DAY 63

"Upon entering a room full of people, you find them saying one thing, doing another, and wishing they were doing a third. . . . The words are secondary and the secrets are primary."

—MIKE NICHOLS

TEXT, SUBTEXT, AND IRONY

Hi Writers,

Text is everything spoken as well as every gesture, entrance, and exit, every silence. The unspoken meaning under text is *subtext*. "I have a headache," might mean in subtext, "I need to end this marriage and don't know how to say it." Subtext entertains and triangulates with an audience by playing a game with what isn't being said. The audience doesn't always have to know exactly what the subtext is, but they enjoy realizing there's a secret in play. Text that is *"on the nose"* lacks subtext. It can at times be effective to be on the nose. For example, if a character has been avoiding saying directly how she feels and then finally states, "I hate you," the audience will be primed to see what reaction this provokes. Moliere's Misanthrope can't abide dancing around opinions nicely; his "on the nose" comments provoke conflict in "polite society."

The audience has *omniscience* when it knows more than the characters.

When we grasp the fate that awaits a character, we discern a double meaning, a subtext, in every exchange. In a mystery we might know the villain before others do. We might discover one character plans to propose marriage before another does. By dramatizing familiar myths, the Greek plays give a double meaning to almost every utterance. Dionysus appears disguised to Pentheus but not to the audience. As the god methodically gives the brash young ruler chance after chance to honor him, we recognize with subtext how Pentheus unknowingly consigns his family to a tragic end.

A character might claim that another has a secret subtext to what s/he is saying, whether or not that's true. Even with people we love most we at times mistake the meaning in what someone says. Friendships can be lost over small misinterpretations of text and subtext. In *Clybourne Park* white characters try not to offend the black couple in their midst, but make things worse. The most overtly racist among them reads false subtext into Lena's comments: "She as much as claimed that there's some kind of, of, of *secret conspiracy*."

With *irony*, subtext is the opposite of text and so gives double meaning to a statement. In David Henry Hwang's *M. Butterfly* male Chinese Opera performer Song impersonates a female. Believing Song to be female, M. Gallimard is smitten with him/her. Gallimard says he usually doesn't like the Puccini opera *Madame Butterfly* because, "I've always seen it played by huge women in so much bad makeup."

> SONG: Bad makeup is not unique to the West.
> GALLIMARD: But, who can believe them?
> SONG: And you believe me?
> GALLIMARD: Absolutely. You were utterly convincing.
> It's the first time—
> SONG: Convincing? As a Japanese woman? The
> Japanese used hundreds of our people for medical
> experiments during the war, you know. But I gather such
> an irony is lost on you.
> GALLIMARD: No! I was about to say, it's the first time
> I've seen the beauty of the story.

Gallimard is unaware of the ironic subtext in this exchange, made even more entertaining for the audience by referring to irony in the text.

SUGGESTIONS FOR THE DAY:

1. Does any character conflict with another by believing the other has a secret subtext?
2. Do we ever have omniscience in your play? How and why?
3. Do any of your characters use irony? How and why?
4. Are your characters being too "on the nose"? Where, why? How might you change that?

Until tomorrow,
Linda

WEEK 9: THOUGHTS AND REMINDERS

- Look for universal themes such as hubris, hamartia, and illusion that might be emerging.

- Most characters aren't static. Consider how they might surprise themselves.

- Imagine characters' movement and sound production in terms of Weight, Speed, Line, and Attitude.

- Do characters' external behaviors change during the play in ways that help illustrate the spine of dramatic action?

- Score the spine of your play like a musical composition to help you plan the scenario.

- Characters collide in the Middle.

- Whether characters change or not, the audience usually hopes change for the better is possible for some.

- Inhabit each character each moment as an actor might.

- If you write a scene quickly, go back through it slowly, sensing each moment as it might occur in performance.

- Vivid words are alive with the sounds, images, smells, and visceral experiences of life.

- Those of us who love writing and words have an obligation to battle the mundane.

- Use metaphor to enliven your audience.

- Characters reveal their pasts as circumstances force them to do so—often bit by bit instead of all at once.

- Revealing the past should help a character evolve into a new understanding of the present.

- Is a character lying about the past? How might this affect your play?

- References to the past must move the action forward.

- Creating subtext can help you generate suspense for the audience.

- Subtext and irony bring an audience into play with you because of what isn't being said.

WEEK 10

SUSPENSIONS AND CRISIS

With more techniques and examples for wrestling with the Middle, you will move the action towards crisis. You consider using foreshadowing to pique audience attention. The roles your characters play slip progressively as they change. You will study choral function—both actual use of chorus and embedding its ancient effects—to create each unit's ethos in the play's musicality.

DAY 64

"[T]he beginning always seems more promising . . . the middle is a timid jumble, and the end is an explosion of fireworks, just like a brief sketch."

—ANTON CHEKHOV

EXPERIMENTING IN THE MIDDLE

Hi Writers,

You will finish your first draft of the Middle in the next two weeks. Portions of the script might be well developed, while others are sketchy. Some units might be narrated, if you can't hear and imagine the dialogue at the moment. Whether or not your play is story-based, your characters' emotions, ideas, behavior and relationships take the foreground. Some dialogue or monologues provide interesting texture but impede forward motion. Don't discard those, but also don't let them distract you from keeping characters' actions necessary and consequential.

We don't even know what the first performance drafts of the 5th century BC Greek plays were, since "official" versions were not decreed until late in the 4th century BC. By the time the official versions were determined all the original playwrights were long deceased. The masterful works by Shakespeare went through the fires of many performances and contributions by his acting company. It's quite likely that each play was revised considerably over the years between first performance and eventual publication after his death.

The Italian Renaissance master Gian Lorenzo Bernini's marble and bronze sculptures did not appear overnight in their perfected form. He made rough drawings to explore dynamics of form. He also "sketched" quickly in three dimensional terra cotta "bozzetti" to record ideas. Once he devised desirable lines and proportions, Bernini used more detailed small terra cotta "modellos" to show a design. From models he and assistants could begin their work on the final sculpture. Bernini made many sketches and considered his design from numerous angles before committing to a final product. This is how I encourage you to approach craft.

SUGGESTIONS FOR THE DAY:

1. Collect and create new episodes, units of beats, dialogue exchanges and monologues you think you might want in the Middle—without worrying over how they fit together.
2. What stake does each character have in the outcome of major conflicts in the Middle?
3. How do characters become more complex, constricted or expanded in the Middle?
4. How do characters contrast with one another for dramatic and theatrical effect?
5. How does the Middle end?
6. Imagine each possibility for the end of the Middle as the top of a ladder. What are the other steps on the ladder?
7. Write out story and character ideas you *don't* want in the Middle.

Until tomorrow,
Linda

HOMEWORK FOR THE WEEK

1. Continue drafting the Middle.

2. Continue collecting new ideas through stream-of consciousness.

3. Experiment with formatting styles to create flow of dialogue.

DAY 65

"A forward is any of a myriad of devices, techniques, tricks, maneuvers, manipulations, appetizers, tantalizers, teasers, that make an audience eager for what's coming up."

—**David Ball**

THE ARROW FLIES FORWARD: FORESHADOWING

Hi Writers,

Physicists speculate that time doesn't have a beginning or end, that it's theoretically possible to visit ourselves in another time. Writers can manipulate time—flashing back or organizing plot points backwards, for example. However, our physical lives begin and then end in what we experience as a linear pattern of growing old. "The arrow flies forward": Physicists acknowledge that is the progression of time as our bodies perceive it. This is a guiding principle in drama. From whatever you have chosen to set the action in motion to its end, the audience subconsciously desires forward movement. If a scenario arranges plot points in a nonlinear or even backwards pattern, such as Harold Pinter's *Betrayal*, the audience's experience is that of dramatic movement from a beginning to an end.

Besides major technical elements like your inciting incident and intrusions, you create forward movement in numerous ways. *Foreshadowing* is one of the most common techniques to maintain "what's next?" The term literally means that the shadow falls in front of a figure—we see the shadow before the whole figure emerges. A writer drops in a teasing reference to something early without giving the full story. Usually you'll mention the item again a second time, revealing a bit more information before the payoff on the third mention. Keep in mind this *rule of three*. There is an expectation in humans for story detail to emerge in three segments. Even the smallest story thread has its own beginning, middle and end. These threads help you bind the tale you're spinning. For example, in *Boy Gets Girl* Theresa mentions her love of sports in her first encounter with Tony. She and porn producer Len discover later this is a shared interest. In the end, her love of baseball wins Theresa a new life as a sports writer.

Flashbacks should move the plot forward even as they go back in time. In *Landscape of the Body*, a prologue on a boat with Betty and policeman Holahan sets up the theme that we're all out at sea and prepares us for the play's fluid structure. We flash back to watch Holahan grill Betty, a suspect in her son's death. Through the play we move in and out of time, meeting the son before his death, gathering clues that lead us to understand what happened. These flashbacks foreshadow future events, so we always feel we're moving forward.

SUGGESTIONS FOR THE DAY:

1. What foreshadowing have you already set up that might be reinforced in intriguing ways?
2. What must happen by the End that you could foreshadow now?
3. Find ways to vary the "forwards" so the audience senses momentum.

Until tomorrow,
Linda

DAY 66

Melville, Stevens, Whitman "give you permission to be excessive, to write your way to an idea even if it means what you are creating is inexcusably long and full of all sorts of distractions and discursions."
—TONY KUSHNER

THE ARROW FLIES FORWARD: SOARING SUSPENSIONS

Hi Writers,

You're wrestling the dramatic action forward, but there's so much you want the characters to say—stories and memories, opinions and discoveries. Imagine a bird flying and then catching a draft of air to soar before flying up again to catch another draft. The bird's active flight has prepared it for that moment. Like the bird, you prepare for the placement of significant moments by giving your characters and your scene forward movement. Characters' monologues spring from necessity and occur after a series of beats that are active through dialogue such as argument, suspense, misunderstandings, or persuasion. When a character launches into a memory or long argument, it is a form of soaring, an activity rather than a stop. Caught up in the action, the audience enjoys the opportunity to ride on the momentum you created.

Another way to think about these monologues in the Middle is the concept of expansion or blossoming. The action moves forward in a linear manner and then it expands in more dimensions when a character speaks from the heart or reacts in anger, opening the fabric of the story into tales from past or future time. The play opens like a flower.

A character's monologue should be active—used to persuade, explain, reach out for sympathy, unleash pent up anger. It will fall, rather than soar, if it's only there as a mouthpiece for your beliefs. Ask yourself: Is this necessary at this time in the play for the character's forward movement? Does this speech contribute to the forward action? Monologues should occur at key moments when characters must make decisions. If you have built the action so we believe there is urgency behind the decision-making, the monologue continues to propel the arrow forward. When we know him and his dilemma well, Hamlet wonders, "To be, or not to be." He becomes more fully human and we reach for him empathically precisely because he "stops" to investigate mortality and choice.

You can interrupt characters' monologues in ways that tantalize an audience and keep the action moving. Entrances, exits, phone calls, another character's anger, or an inconsiderate response—various interruptive devices will make the audience even more interested in hearing what a character has to say and will prolong the feeling of soaring suspension.

SUGGESTIONS FOR THE DAY:

1. For each monologue, ask: Is this necessary and useful for the play's forward movement?
2. Are you interrupting monologues in tantalizing ways that extend the soaring?

Until tomorrow,
Linda

DAY 67

"There is no way on earth that we can order anyone
or ourselves to rally knowledge. It is rather a slow
affair; the body, at the right time and under the proper
circumstances of impeccability, rallies its knowledge
without the intervention of desire."

—Carlos Castaneda

FORMAT NUTS AND BOLTS

Hi Writers,

Today we take a break from theory and play dissection to open the toolbox and look at a few formatting techniques. This gives your subconscious a chance to rally its knowledge. As you proceed through the Middle and approach crisis, your characters are more likely to interrupt one another, speak over one another, and even all talk at once. That contributes to the musical sense of rising intensity and increasing urgency.

The way you format speech can influence actor/director choices for delivery. When you want to convey characters' emotional experiences, hesitancies, confusions and so forth without words, you can separate words on the page with ellipses, dashes, commas, semicolons, and colons. You might use all capital letters and italics for a variety of emphases. You can indicate pauses in various ways, but don't over-control the speech. Avoid using cues such as "(Yells at her.)." Instead, he can say, "I did not!" She can reply, "You don't have to yell at me." If you've written the characters and moments well, good actors will perform it well.

To suggest the flow of a speech, or lack of it, use ellipses (. . .) or dashes. Bring words to full stops. Just. Like. This. Or run words together in stream-of-consciousness without using any punctuation to encourage the actor to keep plunging through the speech like this.

David Mamet places some dialogue in *American Buffalo* in parentheses, "which serve to mark a slight change of outlook on the part of the speaker—perhaps a momentary change to a more introspective regard."

> DON: "You can't live on coffee, Bobby. (And I've told you this before.)

In *TopdogUnderdog*, Suzan-Lori Parks gives characters a beat with no words or action dictated: "This is a place where the figures experience their pure true simple state. While no action or stage business is necessary, directors should fill this moment as they best see fit."

> "Lincoln
> Booth
> Lincoln
> Booth"

You can indicate overlapping or simultaneous speeches in various ways. You might simply indicate in directions that "Nick and Nora's speeches occur simultaneously" and then enter the two speeches, one after the other, leaving it to others to decide how to perform it.

If you want an interruption to happen at specific moments as speeches overlap, you can indicate the point of interruption with a cue like a "/" or an "*" (Parks does this in *Topdog/Underdog*). Or, write one character's speech until the overlap occurs; use a hyphen at the point of interruption and then begin the next character's speech below, perhaps prefacing it with [interrupting].

The dinner scene in *August: Osage County* is set in three columns:

STEVE: I told you, smoke a cigarette and the food comes— KAREN. (*To Barbara*) when's the last time someone mowed the yard around here?	MATTIE FAE. Well, look who decided to show up. I'm sorry we woke you, sweetheart. LITTLE CHARLES. Mom, I'm so Sorry—	IVY. I'm serious if you say anything— VIOLET. You didn't say I couldn't tell people— IVY. I'm telling you now.

In *Clybourne Park*, speeches are side by side in as many as four columns.

ALBERT. *Sorry, sir, my fault!* That was me. That was all my doing.	FRANCINE. *(top of the stairs). That was my fault! I'm sorry!*	BEV. Oh oh oh. What happened? Is everyone all right?	RUSS. *Aw, for crying out out loud!* What the heck is The matter with people? *Bev, darn it all!!*

In *Angels in America, Part One: Millennium Approaches*, Tony Kushner sometimes calls for split scenes in which two couples are onstage in separate settings and gives dialogue first to one couple then another. In Act II, Scene 9, though, Kushner creates the sense of impending crisis by overlapping dialogue between split scenes: "This should be fast and obviously furious; overlapping is fine; the proceedings may be a little confusing but not the final results."

SUGGESTIONS FOR THE DAY:

Experiment with formatting to discover the right "look" and musicality for your play.

Until tomorrow,
Linda

DAY 68

"Theater exists all around us and it is the purpose of formal theater to remind us that this is so."

—John Cage

DEEP STRUCTURE

Hi Writers,

Although the Greek chorus as it was designed in 5th century BC has almost disappeared from dramas, its functions remain deeply embedded in dramatic structure. The chorus of widows in Sally Nemeth's *Mill Fire* reminds us of the broader communal context of one widow's drama. Choruses in Adrienne Kennedy's plays provide repetitions of themes and imagery. The Greek chorus carried much of the exposition and history so characters could focus on immediate action, helped create atmosphere and tone, and provided a musical throughline for both structure and action. Understanding those functions can be useful whether you're creating a realistic fourth wall illusion or a post-modern nonlinear poetic performance.

Today I introduce the chorus and its musical function in general. In the next letter I will overview how the integration of chorus into the action of a Greek drama created a dynamic substructure in the Middle that helps an audience hear, feel, and see the crisis, climax, and conclusion.

Each ancient Greek play follows a typical structural pattern: A prologos is delivered by one or more actors to set up the "problem" and place. The chorus enters dancing and singing in a parodos. A series of agons or episodes (scenes of conflict) follow the parodos, each separated from the other by a choral stasimon (singing and dancing). Usually there are five to seven agons. As the play approaches the height of the conflict, the stasima bleed into the agons until the climactic moment is an explosive blending of characters' dialogue and monologues with choral singing. The play ends with a character and/or the chorus providing some kind of summary commentary as the chorus sings and dances away in an exodus.

Choral songs were chosen from existing music or composed as appropriate to the story. Here is one of the keys to their importance: The music itself (meter, rhythm, ethos, associations) mattered almost as much as the words. This is what is so often lost in contemporary translations of the plays. Each song has its own "*ethos*" or mood, like Sanskrit ragas. For us the influence of a brassy military march by John Phillip Sousa is much different from bagpipes playing "Amazing Grace." Each choral contribution is not just a different song but a musical composition that contributes a particular ethos to the scene and characters as well triangulating associatively with audience memories and feelings.

The Greek chorus sets a mood and tone when they first dance into the theatre. They create transitions in ethos as the action progresses, singing and dancing between as well as within agons. Euripides' *The Bacchae* begins with the nature god Dionysus in disguise, newly arrived in Thebes to punish the city for denying that his mother was impregnated by Zeus and for refusing to honor his divinity. Suddenly men dressed as female bacchantes sing a hymn to Dionysus as they dance into the orchestra with drums, flutes, and possibly cymbals and a kind of saxophone to an ethos we might think of today as exuberant Bollywood. With sounds carried out of Persia and the Middle East and across the Caucasus, the spirit of Dionysus should fill the theatre and resonate viscerally with each person in the audience.

Dionysus disappears. Pentheus, the brash new king, rails against Dionysus. After he exits, the chorus shifts tone into outrage and warning, together with an invocation to the heavens. In this way, the chorus leads us through the action. They drum when Pentheus has his attendants bind Dionysus' hands. Their song after that agon calls upon Dionysus to "quell with death this beast of blood"— now they're an angry, growling mob. They foreshadow future action. Dionysus escapes imprisonment. He will give Pentheus one more chance to recognize the god. The chorus has lifted the play's intensity—the next agon suspends all in the audience and onstage as Dionysus confronts the arrogant king. Pentheus falls into the god's trap. Dionysus tells the Chorus: "Women, our prey now thrashes in the net we threw." The stasimon that follows blends the opening song with excitement for the punishment ahead and ecstasy to follow.

The need for choral effect remains today—displaced, transformed. Characters generate and share ethos as they speak, as they tell stories onstage. Today's playwright modulates mood and rhythm within the play without the benefit of a chorus. Units of beats and short scenes between passages of strong action function musically like the chorus. Secondary characters might be used for the choral function. Fourth wall realism and nonlinear theatre can utilize lessons from the Greek chorus to guide an audience emotionally.

SUGGESTIONS FOR THE DAY:

1. Consider the ethos created by each unit of beats or each scene you have created and in today's writing. Are they in keeping with how you are hoping an audience will feel?
2. Does each ethos serve as substructure to the action?

Until tomorrow,
Linda

DAY 69

"The creative process has more than one kind of expression. There's the part you could show in a movie montage—the furious typing or painting or equation solving where the writer, artist or mathematician accomplishes the output of the creative task. But then there's also the part that happens invisibly, under the surface. That's when the senses are perceiving the world, the mind and heart are thrown into some sort of dissonance, and the soul chooses to respond."
—**DOUGLAS RUSHKOFF**

CHORUS AND CRISIS

Hi Writers,

In the beginning of a Greek drama there is a separation of chorus and characters. The chorus infiltrates agons in the Middle by singing shorter songs. At times it appears to split into parts. When protagonist and antagonist have reached the end of their arguments at crisis there is almost no separation between agon and stasimon. The protagonist's monologue takes the foreground like a pianist playing over an orchestra. The "voices" of the play interrupt and challenge one another. This cacophony or tremendous swelling can go no further.

Your characters create these choral effects as much through how they speak and behave as what they say and do. Something happens at crisis and then climax that is beyond words. As the above quote suggests, "That's when the senses are perceiving the world, the mind and heart are thrown into some sort of dissonance, and the soul chooses to respond." Characters in the throes of distress rarely speak calmly and logically. They interrupt one another in anger, pain, or some kind of excitement. Often they speak all at once—like a symphony orchestra swelling sound together. Physically they often find it difficult to sit or stand still. They might even threaten to harm one another or actually do so. Chekhov calls for a dance party in Act Three of *The Cherry Orchard*. Like the ancient chorus, characters weave in and out of the crisis—the sale of the estate—with interruptions, music, and people in various states of intoxication. Katori Hall utilizes choral function as *The Mountaintop* reaches crisis: The angel Camae tells Martin Luther King, "Let's take you to the mountaintop." "Lightning flickers as images from that fateful day . . . begin to seep through the hotel walls." Camae recites in concert with projected images: "Memphis burning / DC burning / Cities burning / Vietnam burning." Next she "begins to float away into another world. . . . Her voice becoming an echo as the future continues to consume the stage." King speaks from "the deep dark blue of the blackness, trying to take his rightful place in the universe among the stars."

SUGGESTIONS FOR THE DAY:

1. Experiment with creating rising tension and explosive effects as you build into crisis.
2. Study this "fusion" of action and ethos in plays—usually beginning 2/3 into the action.

Until tomorrow,
Linda

DAY 70

"Action, action, action, idea!"

—Ira Glass

ROLES AND SLIPPAGE

Hi Writers,

Characters play roles, not necessarily for devious reasons. We all play roles in relation to other people as social necessity—student one moment, teacher the next, wife or husband and in the next room a parent. Life becomes increasingly complicated when we play several roles at once—sister, mother, teacher, employee. It isn't always easy to play a role demanded by society while at the same time being true to something in ourselves we might think of as "authentic."

When a play begins, the audience assesses—consciously or not—the roles the characters are playing. We wonder how aware the characters are of those roles. We notice changes in their behavior as they play different roles depending on the situation presented to them. It can be comic or tragic and everything in between for characters who cling stubbornly to roles rather than consider change. As each new challenge occurs, characters cling to or question their roles. Perhaps they become confused over what role to play. They can be frightened by the demand that they assume an unfamiliar role.

You're moving into the dramatic crisis of your play's Middle to set up climax and conclusion. Characters rarely simply change 180 degrees when faced with crisis. Your main character and possibly others might go through *"slippage,"* a series of beats and even units of beats in which they lose control of the role they had clung to. As that role is challenged, it slips like a mask; the character grabs it again to readjust, unwilling to let go; it slips again and finally the role has fallen away. "Slippage" gives your characters transitions and adds to the sense of impending crisis. Each major slip catches the audience's attention and gives you the opportunity to express a key idea. Search for the most theatrical, credible and dramatically satisfying ways for characters' roles to slip and for them to respond to that.

Hamlet deliberately plays roles throughout Shakespeare's play; he even creates a play within to catch the conscience of the king. Finally, though, Hamlet accepts his roles as son and prince, facing his adversaries with a monologue about "readiness" that is one of the play's major themes. Terminally ill Violet in *August: Osage County* pulls the masks off her children while she refuses to change. In Tracy Letts's *Bug* both Agnes and Peter progressively lose roles as drugs and paranoia consume them. Finally Agnes releases her "normal" social mask and slips into Peter's beliefs that they're invaded by bugs planted by the government. With no stable roles to play, they burn the room down with themselves inside.

SUGGESTIONS FOR THE DAY:

1. What roles do your characters perform as the play begins and why?
2. Are they conscious of these? How does the audience know that?
3. How and when does the play challenge those roles?
4. Do one or more characters directly challenge their role-playing?
5. Do any characters control changes in their roles during the play? How? Why?
6. Do they lose control of their roles and changes?
7. Are they aware of alternative roles before the play reaches crisis?
8. Will they assume new roles in the conclusion, or will they hide once again behind the old masks?

Until tomorrow,
Linda

WEEK 10: THOUGHTS AND REMINDERS

- Remember that this is the first of many drafts.

- The audience desires a sense of forward movement in a play, regardless of structure.

- The plot and emotional spine don't always move forward in a simple linear manner—characters and plot twist and turn, suspend and soar.

- Foreshadow an event or information without giving away all the information to "forward" a "what's next?" question for the audience.

- When monologues spring from necessity and are actively participating in the plot, they continue to move the play forward while they soar in a suspended state.

- Save as much discovery and information as possible for crisis and climax.

- With formatting you can influence actor/director choices for production.

- Instead of a Greek chorus you use dialogue, monologue, silence, theatricality and a variety of juxtapositions to create and manipulate emotional ethos.

- *How* characters speak and interact—verbally and physically—creates the play's action as much as *what* they say.

- You can create the swell and frenzy of a play's crisis with a manipulation of dramatic techniques; you don't have to rely on words alone.

- Characters play roles. As those roles slip, as characters confront the challenges of losing or changing roles, they progress into crisis.

- Use moments of slippage to place important themes.

UNIT FOUR

DRIVING TO THE END

Y ou are weaving threads of character, plot, theatricality, and theme(s) into crisis, then driving the action through climax into conclusion of the drama. Character decisions and revelations, role slippage and significant turnings occur as necessity and inevitability set in.

WEEK 11

TURNING TO THE END

Y ou create crisis this week and prepare for the climax as you envision the End. You use characters' pasts in their present challenges and decide what the outcomes will be for the crises they face.

DAY 71

"Writing is easy. Finishing is hard."

—UNKNOWN

TURNING POINTS

Hi Writers,

Before the final crisis and climax of a play often there is a slowdown or "pullback" in the tension like a largo movement in a symphony. It might be a false sense of security or the calm before the storm. This is an opportunity to focus on theme, to give more insight into the characters and their relationships. This section might not last as long as a scene. It can be the musical equivalent of a full rest or perhaps even the quiet stop of a symphony as they turn pages between movements. Or, it could be more extended, like the bridge in a song that breaks up repetition of verse/chorus by introducing a variation that is different and yet consistent with the song. You "cleanse the palate" so the final portion of the play will have clarity. With these devices the audience prepares mentally and emotionally for the concluding movement ahead.

In crisis the characters' arguments and feelings spin out of control, approaching and turning towards the apex of disorder, which is the climax. We know this loss of control and reason in life. We want to see how characters handle it, both to recognize ourselves and to gain some understanding of possibilities. The challenges to old roles are most intense. Your main character or ensemble characters are urged to let those roles "slip" away and face decisions without a mask.

At some point acceptance of the crisis must set in to reach the climax. Then decisive action turns events, and leads to resolution (sometimes transformation). Will they, like Violet in *August: Osage County*, force everyone to hear the family's secrets? Or like Agnes in *Bug*, will they choose self-destruction? *Boy Gets Girl* takes a shocking turn into crisis when Theresa discovers Tony broke into her apartment and mutilated her treasured books. We literally recognize crisis with her when she encounters this symbolic rape of her world. Now it seems Tony is capable of anything, even murder. Don't hold back on extreme possibilities for your characters as you imagine what can happen at this crucial turning point. Explore new emotional and psychological territory for them.

SUGGESTIONS FOR THE DAY:

1. Sketch the decision (or decisions) that must be made in crisis by the character(s) driving the spine of the action.
2. How can you "show" crisis to us theatrically, not just with words?

Until tomorrow,
Linda

HOMEWORK FOR THE WEEK

1. Finish the Middle.

2. Focus on crisis, characters, theatricality, language, theme(s)

3. Prepare for climax and conclusion.

DAY 72

*"A dreamer is one who can only find his way by moonlight
and his punishment is that he sees the dawn before the
rest of the world."*

—Oscar Wilde

GLIMPSING THE END

Hi Writers,

Envision your play's probable End, including alternatives you sketched to
sustain unpredictability. This will help you make decisions about the construction of crisis in the Middle. Tracing backwards you can test plot logic
and review character turns. Inhabiting the End now can refresh your enthusiasm for the play. With fewer than three weeks to go, remember why
you care about this idea and these characters. The End contains theme(s)
you want to express and rounds off human interaction in a way that is
plausible and meaningful. For Horton Foote a play's resolution was a moment of transcending the mundane, of rising above tragedy or life's petti-
ness. Let your excitement for the play's "soul" nourish you.

A resolution should be aesthetically and logically satisfying. It can
mean surrendering an old role/identity, emerging from the chrysalis, transformation through recognition, death/loss, multiple marriages, defeating a
foe, a radical change in family/relationship dynamics, or a sad return to
same old same old but this time with more awareness. Conclusions vary.
Comedies have a "happy" ending in which all is well after the storms pass
over, except for a "dark" comedy like *The Misanthrope*, that resolves with an
unhappy protagonist. Plays can end abruptly at the height of an argument
or when the stage is littered with corpses. Or, they can take time to return
to a place of calm, as in Kalidasa's Sanskrit classic *The Sign of Shakuntala*.

Aristotle admired *Oedipus Rex* because the protagonist must suffer,
learn, and transform in the end, perhaps prompting audience members to
go through a wrenching personal emotional journey (catharsis) themselves.
Antigone doesn't transform; she dies and her antagonist Creon transforms
as a result. David Mamet teases the audience for *American Buffalo* with

characters plotting a theft they don't go through with due to events outside their control. Mamet uses a ticking clock device to keep the audience hooked into the action as the time for the theft approaches, and then he twists expectation. No character changes. Deanna Jent's *Falling* doesn't end with a tidy solution for a family whose autistic son is becoming a man increasingly difficult to have in the home. Should they institutionalize him or continue to live with the challenges he presents? The audience realizes that families faced with this situation live in genuine dilemma.

SUGGESTIONS FOR THE DAY:

1. If a major character doesn't undergo self-examination and change as a result of the play's struggles—why not?
2. What experience do you want in the End for the audience, and why?
3. Envision the final moment before curtain. Describe the expressions on each character's face.

Until tomorrow,
Linda

DAY 73

"In a good play every speech should be as fully flavoured as a nut or apple."

—JOHN M. SYNGE,
Preface to *The Playboy of the Western World*

WORDS TO HAVE A WAY WITH

Hi Writers,

While you agonize over devising the Middle and leading us into crisis and climax, relax your rational mind by playing with figurative language. Have fun with words any day, every day when the going gets tough. Write to enjoy yourself. Following are terms and classifications you might find useful for your writer's toolbox:

Mimetic words: When you say or hear them you see, feel and smell what they refer to. With "oily" you can have several sensations at once from such a small word.

Onomatopoetic words sound like their referents: "Buzz," "sigh," "gulp." The word "sing" is a tiny song in itself.

Most of the time people use *denotative* words that simply identify a person or a thing: "He's a lawyer." That is "on the nose." There's no triangle, no work for the imagination. *Connotative* speech, on the other hand, implies more of a feeling or attitude about a person: "She's a weasel," "They're a couple of trolls."

You probably use *metonymy* often without knowing the name for it: "Live by the sword, die by the sword." "Hoisted on his own petard." "Cooked her own goose." With metonymy you evoke an idea with an associated term. You combine metaphor and/or symbol with verbal action.

Synecdoche is related to metonymy; again, it's an uncommon term for a common language choice in which you use a broader term for something specific. "The law" designates a policeman. Some use "The Man" for whoever represents corporate and/or political power.

Paraprosdokian refers to a sentence in which the latter part twists or surprises in a way that causes a reinterpretation of the first part. "I've had a perfectly wonderful evening, but this wasn't it." (Groucho Marx)

SUGGESTIONS FOR THE DAY:

1. Throw open the dictionary and choose words at random. Say the words out loud, use them in sentences, rhymes, stream-of-consciousness stories, or poems.

2. Resurrect words that have fallen out of common usage. Consider these obsolete English words you can play with and perhaps use: "Jargogle"— to confuse, jumble; "brabble"—to quarrel about trifles, especially to quarrel noisily; "freck"—to move swiftly or nimbly.

3. Can any of your characters use silly words, unusual words, words that are mimetic, onomatopoetic, connotative?

Until tomorrow,
Linda

DAY 74

"You were wild once. Don't let them tame you."
—ISADORA DUNCAN

WHERE THE WILD THINGS ARE

Hi Writers,

At this stage in the process you can be overly concerned about dramatic rules, page numbers, and the fine points of construction. If they impede your putting words on the page, shake them off and let your imagination gallop across the hills. This draft will be whatever pages it needs to be to get you through it. You have revisions ahead for tuning and shaping. And even then your untamed imagination should play freely.

Let your characters go to extremes as you approach the End—if you hold them too tightly now they won't help you find the heights and depths of the story. They should probe and push each other's buttons for crisis and climax. One or more should strip another of safety and pretense. How do they respond when they lose self-control and/or lose control of their environment? We in the audience should see ourselves in them—at our best and at our worst. Will they show us how to handle crisis? Or will they remind us how *not* to behave? Will they surprise us with their reactions and tactics? As you reach crisis and climax the audience needs to feel you've gone farther with story and character behavior than we could imagine. Therefore, let this first draft be as untamed as possible.

The "wildness" of Horton Foote's imagination doesn't result in people yelling at each other onstage so much as balancing between plot elements that go to the limit and characters powerless at the other extreme. David Henry Hwang sets *F.O.B.* in the back room of a Chinese-American restaurant. In the beginning assimilated Grace and "fresh off the boat" Steve converse in realistic dialogue. As their arguments delve into themes we encounter in other plays by Hwang (Chinese/American identity, ethnic stereotypes and cultural "authenticity") the characters enact mythic/heroic characters Chinese Opera-style. Becoming Fu Mu Lan, "the girl who takes her father's place in battle" from Maxine Hong Kingston's *The*

Woman Warrior, Grace strikes pots together to indicate changes in speaker. Steve transforms into Gwan Gung, "the god of fights and writers" from Frank Chin's *Gee, Pop*. The play bursts from realism into lyric theatricality.

SUGGESTIONS FOR THE DAY:

1. How do your characters probe to find the buttons to push in each other to generate crisis and climax?
2. How do they push those buttons?
3. Are you aware of holding your imagination back, self-censoring? If so, why?
4. If you find it difficult to explore characters' possible actions and reactions within script format, write speeches and dialogue separately in stream-of-consciousness. Just let everything rip without a voice cautioning, "Oh, no, she can't say that!"

Until tomorrow,
Linda

DAY 75

> *"What's Hecuba to him, or he to Hecuba,*
> *That he should weep for her? What would he do*
> *Had he the motive and the cue for passion*
> *That I have?"*
>
> —**WILLIAM SHAKESPEARE,** *Hamlet*

WHO WILL WEEP FOR HECUBA?

Hi Writers,

Entangled in his personal passion for revenge, Hamlet can't imagine feeling anything for a character in a fictional story—not even for Hecuba, the Queen of Troy, forced to watch as her entire family was either slaughtered or enslaved, and as she awaited her own slavery. Rather than ask visiting

Players to perform a play about Hecuba, Hamlet devises for them a pantomime re-enacting what his Father's Ghost told him were the details of his brother Claudius's fratricide. Hamlet hopes Claudius's reaction to that pantomime will betray his guilt. This play within Shakespeare's play, known as "The Mousetrap," is set "to catch the conscience of a king."

Does a story have to be narrowly personal to make us feel something? We hope not, for that would place great limitations on storytelling. And yet, there should be something with a broad general reach in your theme(s) as well as your characters and their fates, whether comic or tragic or anything in between, to "catch the conscience" of the audience.

If you want the audience to think more than feel, through disruptive ("estranging") devices such as media projections and direct address to the audience popularized by Berthold Brecht, you still have an idea for what mood you want the audience to enter by the end, what thoughts you want them to take home. You might be attempting both to move an audience emotionally and to inspire them to think about important human issues. Moliere's *The Imaginary Invalid* exposes human traits that can be recognized across cultures and time. An audience leaves that comedy satisfied from having laughed but also pondering its message of narcissistic hypochondriacs and con men that prey on them, and wondering if they recognized themselves or someone they know in the play.

SUGGESTIONS FOR THE DAY:

1. What feelings and thoughts do you want the audience to have at the end of your play?
2. Be specific for how you want the audience to feel and think about each character. This will help you with the tone and plot/scenario solutions in the final pages.
3. Trace through your scenario the plot points, speeches, and dialogue that should most acutely engage the audience in caring about the outcome for each character.

Until tomorrow,
Linda

DAY 76

"A book's last third takes ten percent of the time. That's not confidence; it's that the alternatives have been narrowed down."

—Joseph Heller

IT ALL COMES TOGETHER

Hi Writers,

All the drama and themes you've devised come together and peak at climax. There is no one way to approach or design the climax. It doesn't have to be a cacophony of full orchestra or all the characters going at each other at once. Imagine the swell of an orchestra for crisis and then an extended phrase of trembling strings for climax, for example. Think of the climax as being like a close score or tie going into the last two minutes of a football game—the game remains open for suspense and unpredictability, but the potential for its outcome is limited. While you're pulling "it" together, you continue to suspend the final outcome of the action or the final shape of your aesthetic resolution. Keep one or two alternative conclusions active until the final beats.

What will happen to the cherry orchard? The question hovers in the climax of Chekhov's play with the unresolved hopes, aspirations, pasts and futures of all the characters. "I bought it," Lopahin reveals—and the End begins. Even as he claims ownership of the estate, Lopahin is re-imagining himself, deciding whether or not to propose to Varya and how to treat the former owners as he assumes his new role, his new mask as lord of the manor. At climax the audience still can't be certain what will happen to the cherry orchard.

Use theatrical elements to elevate the effect of the climax. Hamlet is alone in a storm-tossed boat on the North Sea as his crisis reaches climax. (Technically he's on an empty stage; the audience imagines the metaphorical setting.) He has discovered that Claudius sent him on this trip to have him murdered. Hamlet cleverly rescues himself. He has to devise a new way of behaving, though, a new tactic, since his old device of playing the madman hasn't helped him prevail. He'll return, ready for what comes his way, realizing he can't control the outcome. Hamlet will behave like a prince at last, even if it means his death. The image of Hamlet by himself "at sea" suggests how each of us faces key decisions alone, with no support from the material world.

SUGGESTIONS FOR THE DAY:

1. What are the plot threads and theme(s) that "come together" at climax? Clarify what is hanging in the balance for your characters, especially the main character—at climax.
2. Trace plot points that make the climax a logical outcome for the crisis.
3. Articulate what remains unresolved—what you're leaving for the End.

Until tomorrow,
Linda

DAY 77

"The world is made up of stories, not atoms."
—**MURIEL RUKEYSER**

THE PAST IN CRISIS, CLIMAX, AND CONCLUSION

Hi Writers,

Your characters' pasts are with them in the present. Though we experience time as the arrow flying forward, our minds shift back into remembered stories that have become part and parcel of our identities. We try to unburden ourselves of these endless loops from the past. The older we get, some stories become locked into a static frame like an old photo. Or—we bury them, transform them, diminish them, continue to try to make sense of them, celebrate them. Often the past is a crucial element in the inciting incident as well as crisis, climax and conclusion of a play. If Agamemnon hadn't sacrificed his first-born child, his wife wouldn't be waiting to kill him. Clytemnestra won't let go of the past. Her son Orestes avenges his father's death when he reaches manhood by killing his mother. In the third of the Oresteia trilogy, Athena has the last word by transforming the Furies that haunt Orestes for matricide and releasing the Ghost of Clytemnestra from her grip on revenge. The goddess resolves the legacy of memory and past deeds by instituting a new civil order. On a grand scale, this oldest drama we have in script form utilizes a basic pattern many plays follow: Past deeds and memories drive an action until something must change. In this great trilogy the change occurs within main characters, the social order, and the realm of spirit.

At the apex of the action the past can spill out in the form of previously repressed memories as well as deliberately withheld secrets that affect the outcome of the drama. Devastating family secrets emerge by the end of *August: Osage County*. Rather than transform that family into something better than before, revelations of secrets further damage an already dysfunctional household and leave the terminally ill matriarch alone to die. Ibsen's Nora in *A Doll's House* once forged her father's signature on a loan and has kept that secret to protect her husband. When the secret comes out, it precipitates crisis and climax. Her husband's response to the truth and his treatment of her in the aftermath lead Nora to revise her view of self and marriage. She decides to leave her family and her past to create a new self.

Revelations about the past that come out in crisis and climax can be used to punish, persuade, explain, confess, shock, console, heal—and more. Characters make revelations only because the previous action has forced them to, through necessity. And those revelations themselves, which might not be reliable, must play an active role in forcing the action forward. Even in the End, revelations about the past can sound the final active note.

Early in *Who's Afraid of Virginia Woolf?* George sets up the argument and theme from the past that will dominate his tangles with Martha during the play: "Don't start on the kid," he warns her. She defies him by telling her guests they have a son. George thwarts her creation of a false past and present by pretending that someone delivered a telegram informing them the son is dead. When Martha demands to see the telegram, George destroys not only their argument in this play but presumably Martha's use of the fictional son to sow dissent: "I ate it."

As characters conflict about the past, consider the reliability—or not—of memory. The Japanese story "Rashomon," adapted for theatre and film, depicts three characters' distinctly different memories of an incident. Not only are some facts different, but more importantly their interpretations of the event and of the other characters' actions differ. Just because a character tells a story a certain way, is it possible s/he's lying or that her memory is radically different from another's?

SUGGESTIONS FOR THE DAY:

What roles do the past and memory—including reliability and necessity—play in forging the crisis, climax and conclusion of your play?

Until tomorrow,
Linda

WEEK 11: THOUGHTS AND REMINDERS

- If you are struggling with the Middle, look ahead to crisis and climax to clarify your goals.

- In crisis the characters' arguments and feelings spin out of control, approaching the apex of disorder, which is the climax.

- Acceptance of the crisis sets in at the climax. Then decisive action turns events and leads to resolution.

- Envisioning and inhabiting your End can help you clarify the Middle as well as refresh your enthusiasm for the play.

- Write about each major character's choices at climax to articulate the action for yourself.

- The concluding episode of the play should be consistent with what you want the audience to take from the experience of a performance.

- Have fun with words every day; write to enjoy yourself.

- Let your inner wild child romp, especially in the first draft, while you explore the extremes of characters and plot points.

- What feelings do you want your audience to have for your characters? What feelings do *you* have for them?

- Trace through your scenario the plot points, speeches and dialogue that should most acutely engage the audience in caring about the outcome for each character.

- While you're pulling "it" together for the climax, you continue to suspend the final outcome of the action.

- Know what alternatives remain for each character at the moment of climax.

- Consider the roles of past and memory—including reliability and necessity—in forging the crisis, climax and end.

<u>WEEK 12</u>

CLIMAX AND DECISIONS

You will identify plot and character threads you created in past weeks and decide how to tie them up in conclusion. You will review your writing for stage movements, logic, and plausibility while identifying the play's shape as you approach the final units.

DAY 78

"Never underestimate the power of the repeating image."
—David Ball

FOLLOWING THE THREADS

Hi Writers,

Theseus slew the Minotaur and escaped its labyrinthine lair with a thread he'd trailed behind. Princess Ariadne obtained the thread for him from a male artist. An earlier version of that myth honors Ariadne as the goddess of Crete who knew about threads, facing beasts and liberation—until she fell for Theseus. She gave him the thread as a token of love, trust and knowledge. He took her from Crete and then abandoned her. Dionysus fell in love with her and made her his queen. When Ariadne died he threw her crown into the heavens, where it became the Seven Sisters constellation. The world is indeed made up of stories and twists of fate.

With the thickening of the play at climax you're in the heart of your labyrinth. Review the threads you've laid out, some consciously, others by happy chance. One or more should play a role in the climax and others should be involved as the action "falls" and/or transcends through conclusion. *Role-playing and pretense* are commonly used threads. Hamlet pretends to be "mad" in hopes that his antic ways will help him learn whether or not Claudius really killed his father. It leads to tragic consequences. In Shakespeare's comedies women pretend to be men to survive and to unearth truths. "Pretense" itself becomes a theme, played out in dialogue, costume, and physical action. The drama can't end "happily" until all characters have dropped their disguises.

Repetition is an age-old component of storytelling, both for the singer of tales and the audience. People rarely remember something they hear only once. More to the point, an audience subconsciously doesn't give much import to a one-time mention. At least two and preferably three mentions make the information or image "stick" and signal its importance. When you wait until climax or conclusion for the third use of the same reference—whether it's an image, information or theatrical element—you signal that your play is threading its way to a satisfying End. On the other hand, you might discover you have repeated phrases, images, or theatrical elements that shouldn't be given importance or that play no role in your dramatic conclusion. Note that for correction in rewriting.

Slightly alter each reference. You can repeat more than three times if each is fresh. In *Boy Gets Girl*, Theresa loves literature. With Tony and her boss she mentions writers she admires, but neither recognizes the name. This tells us Theresa's interests and shows she is isolated from like minds. Literature is a "thread" that takes us into the heart of the drama. When Tony ruins Theresa's books this thread manifest theatrically makes crisis and climax vivid.

SUGGESTIONS FOR THE DAY:

Review the plot points and threads that are congruent with your theme(s) and central to the action. Note their placement in the action. How are you helping the audience follow them?

Until tomorrow,
Linda

HOMEWORK FOR THE WEEK

1. Review threads for logic, consistency, resolution, and repetitions.
2. Review and fill out stage directions for logic, consistency, and plausibility.
3. Plan, prepare, write to finish next week.

DAY 79

"The professional writer is not necessarily one who makes a lot of money, but one who can control his inspiration."

—Sam Smiley

MORE NUTS, MORE BOLTS

Hi Writers,

Step back now and then to tinker with simple mechanics such as filling out stage directions. Often in writing dialogue and monologues you skip over articulating stage directions because you can see what's happening in your mind's eye. That's fine if it's crucial to your process. Stage directions are for you, though, not just the audience. Observing your characters in brief narrative helps you retain a sense of "stage time." Follow people, see them clearly, describe where they are and what they are doing without being as specific as "she crosses from up right to down left." You'll gain a clearer grasp of a scene's dynamics. You can edit in your final draft.

Stage directions didn't appear in plays in any meaningful way until late in the nineteenth century. Lighting technology was so primitive (daylight or light by candles and oil) that for the most part actors took fixed places on stage and spoke from there. They would enter or exit, and they might move around a bit to adjust to one another, but they didn't create the "stage pictures" we see today. Once gaslight and then electricity entered the scene, what we think of as "modern" plays and staging evolved. Actors and directors could create stage pictures and stage movement that looked like "real" people moving around as they might in "real" living rooms. Now you craft some staging in a way that's new in the history of theatre. Even if you're comfortable with leaving staging decisions to a director, you see your play in the little theatre of your mind. Through directions you might suggest the flavor of the moment, as Lauren Gunderson does with the opening of *Emilie*: "*(Blackness. Then a single light. EMILIE is in this light. She is a little stunned to be here. She breathes—also stunning.)*"

Study the vivid character detail in George Bernard Shaw's preface to *The Doctor's Dilemma*: "On the 15th June 1903, in the early forenoon, a medical student, surname Redpenny, Christian name unknown and of no importance, sits at work in a doctor's consulting-room. He devils for the doctor by answering his letters, acting as his domestic laboratory assistant, and making himself indispensable generally, in return for unspecified advantages involved by intimate intercourse with a leader of his profession, and amounting to an informal apprenticeship and a temporary affiliation. Redpenny is not proud, and will do anything he is asked without reservation of his personal dignity if he is asked in a fellow-creaturely way. He is a wide-open-eyed, ready, credulous, friendly, hasty youth, with his hair and clothes in reluctant transition from the untidy boy to the tidy doctor."

For the setting of *The Piano Lesson*, August Wilson mingles tone and character information with basics: "The action of the play takes place in the kitchen and parlor of the house where Doaker Charles lives with his niece, Berniece, and her eleven-year-old daughter, Maretha. The house is sparsely furnished, and although there is evidence of a woman's touch, there is a lack of warmth and vigor. Berniece and Maretha occupy the upstairs rooms. Doaker's room is prominent and opens onto the kitchen. Dominating the parlor is an old upright piano. On the legs of the piano, carved in the manner of African sculpture, are mask-like figures resembling totems. The carvings are rendered with a grace and power of invention that lifts them out of the realm of craftsmanship and into the realm of art. At left is a staircase leading to the upstairs."

SUGGESTIONS FOR THE DAY:

Review the play to fill out directions for logic, consistency, and plausibility so you're fully connected with the character movements and stage life.

Until tomorrow,
Linda

DAY 80

"That elusive hovering between tragedy and comedy that marks [Chekhov's] work is in fact the first murmuring of a characteristically modern consciousness."

—Lena Lencek

PUTTING AN END TO IT

Hi Writers,

Traditional comedies and melodramas end "happily," with people compatibly coupled off and no outstanding problems remaining. A more thoughtful comedy such as Moliere's *Tartuffe* concludes with a villain ousted and the protagonist acknowledging his own blindness. In Lope de Vega's *Fuente Ovejuna* (usually titled *The Sheep Well* though it means "Bee Spring") women find the courage their men lack and triumph over oppressors. Tragedies might end with the protagonist in exile after achieving inner knowledge, unrelenting destruction of all due to the misdeeds of one individual, or perhaps a resolution left to a god's decision due to human inability to compromise.

With the "modern consciousness," one set of issues might be resolved while another set is left open. The "disquiet" that hovers at the end of Chekhov's plays is present in Beckett's work. We're left with dissonance at the conclusions of *Clybourne Park*; *Who's Afraid of Virginia Woolf?*; and *Mud, River, Stone*, among many others. You complete "enough" of the challenges that have consumed characters and driven the action. We didn't see Jessie's story before she decided to kill herself in *'night, Mother* and we won't see what happens after she does. However, we are satisfied that this is the end of a dramatic slice of that larger story.

Just as the Greek choral function now is embedded in a play's musical construction, a practice known as "*deus ex machina*" (god entering via machine) is an ancestor to modern consciousness. In Aeschylus's *Oresteia*, goddess Athena resolves dilemma by decreeing that civil law will replace vengeance. The goddess shows how to think and behave when people can't resolve conflict for themselves. (Now the term refers to an ending in which someone appears out of the blue to resolve difficulty in an illogical and unsatisfying manner.) Today when you leave an audience with resolution and some dissonance, you invite people to think for themselves. Instead of showing how a goddess would handle a situation, you ask, "What should you do?"

If you are interweaving multiple plotlines, you can bring them into conclusion in many different ways. Assign priorities. The resolution to minor plotlines should serve rather than overshadow the primary drama. It is most satisfying aesthetically if you resolve the least important one first—perhaps as you bring the Middle into crisis and climax. Usually it's best to tease out the major plotline for the final ending beats. An exception to that would be to save a small subplot, like a silly romance, for the finale—that can provide a comic punch.

SUGGESTIONS FOR THE DAY:

Study your plan for the conclusion. Is it forced or organic? Clichéd? Surprising? Logical?

Until tomorrow,
Linda

DAY 81

"I write because I don't know what I think until I read what I say."

—**FLANNERY O'CONNOR**

BEGINNING TO END

Hi Writers,

What is the shape of your play? The standard pattern for a drama is that you set it up, build it until the action reaches crisis and climax, and then resolve it in some sort of payoff. If you are telling a joke, the payoff is the punch line. A play's End is, in a sense, its punch line. Some dramatic structures look like a "ladder": setup, buildup to climax, and payoff with falling intensity at conclusion. Others undulate, gradually reaching a peak. They might end with that peak and little in the way of "falling" (as does *Bug*), or they may slowly taper like *The Cherry Orchard*. Within those shapes are numerous subsets. In fact, we might say that every play is its own subset because each is different from any other. Following are formal designs that might be applied to plays with storylines as well as less conventional theatre experiences:

Order/Disorder. The action begins with a world that seems to be in "*order.*" The inciting incident and other dramatic intrusions disrupt that order, splintering, questioning, challenging, and criticizing it through the Middle. While characters wrestle to bring the world back into order, it's impossible. In the End a new kind of "order" takes shape. After the chaotic disruption of the third act's conflicts, life for Uncle Vanya will be worse. More often than not, though, there is *disorder* from the start. Nora's home life as *A Doll's House* begins appears perfect, but underneath festers not only a secret but a marriage badly in need of challenge.

Thesis/Antithesis/Synthesis. T*hesis* (Clytemnestra kills her husband in revenge), is met with *antithesis* (Clytemnestra's son avenges his father by killing his mother). The result is *synthesis* (Athena's judgment that civil justice will replace revenge). Or, that pattern can lead to destruction. In *Medea* Jason's thesis is that now that he has returned home to lead his people he should marry a princess from his own tribe, turning aside the foreigner (Medea) he brought from the Caucasus. Medea's opposition is the antithesis. She and her sons by Jason will be homeless, the boys will be illegitimate, and the best they can hope for is slavery. She murders the boys, kills the princess, and commits suicide as the tragic synthesis. Also, synthesis can mediate polarities: Philoctetes and his bow will help the Greeks defeat the Trojans and then Odysseus will return the wounded warrior to his home.

SUGGESTIONS FOR THE DAY:

1. How do you describe the overall shape of your play using the terms above?

2. Review the play's spine, musicality and plot logic. What needs to be tied

up (or deliberately left hanging) in the end?

3. Does the Beginning logically and thematically set up the End?

Until tomorrow,
Linda

DAY 82

"There's a really nice moment in the life of a piece of writing where the writer starts to get a feeling of it outgrowing him—or he starts to see it having a life of its own that doesn't have anything to do with his ego or his desire to 'be a good writer.'"

—GEORGE SAUNDERS

WHO'S READY FOR A CLOSEUP?

Hi Writers,

Close ups, medium shots, and long shots direct the viewer's eyes, control story focus, and vary visual composition in film and television. A play is a fluid series of images and a linear arrangement of words and characters' feelings. You are the architect of these arrangements that guide how an audience is to look, listen, and respond, not just generally but also specifically. As you write you assume a focus for each beat and you should vary the foci. Although the audience can see the entire stage, you want them to pay close attention to a speaker at one moment, and then perhaps focus on a couple engaged in dialogue, or in another see all the characters arguing. Transitions and juxtapositions such as entrances, exits, and interruptions with speech and sound keep an audience alert. *Ma Rainey* utilizes three spaces—the downstairs room where black musicians congregate, the mid-level recording studio that is Ma's domain, and a higher production booth where a white producer reigns. At times the focus is on one space while at other times the audience views action in all three.

Combine camera terms with *background and foreground* compositions. Caravaggio placed subjects against black or simple backgrounds
to give full attention to humans. In his film *The Birds* Alfred Hitchcock
juxtaposed a vulnerable woman against a background depicting human
destruction of the environment. Hamlet's "Mousetrap" play-within first
takes the foreground against the assembled court, but the focus shifts to
Claudius and Hamlet as the play catches the conscience of the king. Decide what everyone onstage is doing no matter who is speaking and know
why you've made that decision.

These ideas about focus might assist your choices in writing the very
final beats. There is no one "right" focus. You can end "close on" one
character like Mama in *'night, Mother* or a long shot of all the characters
as in a Shakespearean comedy. That final image is your "last word" about
your tale.

SUGGESTIONS FOR THE DAY:

1. Experiment with angles of vision and composition as you review what
   you've written and create the key components in the final third of the
   script.
2. Study what you're calling for as background and foreground, unit by
   unit.
3. How will your final beats be aesthetically and logically consistent with
   your use of background and foreground earlier in the play—and yet
   provide a surprising twist?

Until tomorrow,
Linda

DAY 83

"I had to create an equivalent for what I felt about what I was looking at—not copy it."

—GEORGIA O'KEEFFE

ON THE MATTER OF STYLE . . .

Hi Writers,

If anyone asks you to describe the style of your play, tell them, "It's my style." An artist's style is an extension of the artist, not an imitation of others. You can tell them the genre (tragedy? comedy? dramedy? melodrama? agit-prop?). You might place it within a certain type of drama (drawing room, character study, interview montage, family in crisis). You might mention a writer with a style "like" yours— but don't diminish your own voice. You are finding and fashioning your voice as you write. The composer Sibelius considered himself a modernist but didn't "fit" with contemporaries Schoenberg and Stravinsky. He invented his own musical structures and orchestrations.

Your style can't be fully "like" any other because it is your own distinct voice. "I don't want realism," Tennessee Williams wrote. "I want magic. Yes, yes, magic! I try to give that to people. I misrepresent things to them. I don't tell the truth, I tell what ought to be the truth. And if that's sinful, then let me be damned for it!" Pay attention to details in other artists so you can train the microscope onto your work. Claim your own style— step back to understand it objectively, be honest with yourself about your tendencies for better or worse. Is there a difference between the voice you use in conversation with trusted friends and the voice you can hear as you read your work? They might be similar, although the written style probably is more heightened, dense and selective. Commit to improving aspects that aren't up to your standards and celebrate what delights you.

There should be consistency to the style of your play. We shouldn't have the impression that one person began it and then dropped out while an entirely different person took over. Consistency doesn't mean conformity or simplicity. The exuberance of Tony Kushner's rich imagination allows great variety in subject matter, tone, vocabulary, and every other tool a writer brings to bear. Nor does consistency mean that each play you write should somehow be like every other. Stretch and challenge yourself, free your subconscious. Though Adrienne Kennedy's plays vary, they share stylistic similarities; Robert Brustein calls them "strong dreams that reveal us in our most vulnerable moments." Themes and images recur, although imagined anew with each creation: Liberation/oppression, feminism, the black church, trust and violations of trust, owls, popular iconography, canonical literature, the African-American family, love.

SUGGESTIONS FOR THE DAY:

Become familiar with your own voice, your style—give your style unconditional love while being willing to tackle what can be improved.

Until tomorrow,
Linda

DAY 84

"The desire to put perfect words in people's mouths comes from never feeling resolved about words I've actually said."

—**Madeleine George**

LAST WORDS ABOUT WORDS

Hi Writers,

The words characters use in the conclusion can make your themes vivid. Was this language foreshadowed earlier in the play, perhaps as early as the beginning? Does it echo or creatively twist on the language at the beginning? Who or what will have the final words in the conclusion of your play? The focus should be on the person(s) and ideas at the center of it.

In the prologue to *August: Osage County*, Beverly quotes T.S. Eliot

("Life is very long") and John Berryman ("The world is gradually becoming a place where I do not care to be anymore"). He disappears in Act I and drowns himself. The family unravels throughout the play. At play's end, Beverly's terminally ill wife chants "and then you're gone" while her maid recites Eliot ("This is the way the world ends"). *Boy Gets Girl* begins with the wordless way Tony and Theresa assess one another when they meet. The difference between how men and women look at each other is one of the play's major themes. In the final scene in her apartment, Theresa's colleague asks if he should turn out the light. She responds, "No. . . . In case he's watching. I don't want him to know I've left." In those final words she echoes the theme of "watching," continues her justifiable paranoia, and closes this slice of her dramatic story.

Sometimes the lack of words at the end of a play can be telling. When words aren't present, especially at the end, their very absence is a kind of presence. After blustering through *Red*, Rothko is speechless when the play concludes. This signals that something in him has changed. He's uncertain and needs to chart new territory. *Old Times* concludes with a long wordless sequence among Pinter's three characters. The audience watches, hearing silence, remembering what has gone before.

In the final moments of *The Cherry Orchard*, Lopahin and the aristocrats have left. They thought ailing elderly servant Fiers, a living symbol of the old feudal system, had gone to the hospital. Instead, they forgot him. Lying down to die in the abandoned house, Fiers mutters, "Life has gone by, as if I hadn't lived at all. . . . nothing is left." The play concludes famously with theatrical elements that have the final word on its themes: "There is a far-off sound as if out of the sky, the sound of a snapped string, dying away, sad. A stillness falls, and there is only the thud of an ax on a tree, far away in the orchard."

SUGGESTIONS FOR THE DAY:

1. Who or what will have the final words in the conclusion of your play? Why?
2. How might words or silence in your conclusion relate to the Beginning?

Until tomorrow,
Linda

WEEK 12: THOUGHTS AND REMINDERS

- Review the threads you've laid out.

- Are you using repetition to thread through the play? The magic of three?

- Articulate stage directions.

- What do you want an audience to carry away from your play's conclusion?

- What is the shape of your play?

- Does the Beginning logically and thematically set up the End?

- Become familiar with your own voice, your style—give your style unconditional love while being willing to tackle what can be improved.

- Who or what will have the final words in the conclusion of your play? The focus should be on the person(s) and ideas at the center of it.

- Consider how the words—or silence—you choose for the End relate to what you chose for the Beginning.

THE FINAL CURTAIN

ENDING THE DRAMA

- Polyvalent themes
- Tying together plot points, themes
- Reviewing with sound off
- End of first draft—soon another beginning
- Finish the play by weaving together and tying off threads of plot points and themes

DAY 85

"This world is full of conflicts and full of things that cannot be reconciled but there are moments when we can transcend the dualistic system and reconcile and embrace the whole mess and that is what I mean by Hallelujah."
—**Leonard Cohen**

IT'S NOT JUST PERSONAL

Hi Writers,

A theme that has impact in *personal, social* and *universal* ways is "polyvalent." Some plays reconcile these three dimensions to find Cohen's transcendent "Hallelujah" moment, although that doesn't always mean a "happy" ending. Vi in *August: Osage County* demands that family secrets be told. A dominant theme in that play is the importance and dangers of telling the truth. Vi's demand for truth affects each person in her family differently. At the *personal* level revelations of family secrets can be devastating, which perhaps questions the notion that we should all be honest. And yet, everyone in that family was harmed by the truth's being covered through the years. There is a *social* plane to Vi's truth-telling as well—it has meaning for groups and not just individuals as the entire family "unit" is blown apart and forever changed.

Truth-telling is a theme with nearly *universal* resonance because it can be extended to social groups beyond families, to nations, to the globe. What truths are too many humans today avoiding and denying? Are they best left alone or could truth help humanity, improve the planet? If the Roman dramatist Seneca were writing *August: Osage County*, the trees outside Vi's house would weep in the end, the house itself heave and crumble, the earth split open. Today's playwrights rarely break the boundaries of "reality" so extravagantly as Seneca, but they can invite us to think that grandly about universal implications.

Cheryl West's *Pullman Porter Blues* dramatizes the men and women who worked on the railroad's Pullman cars. By including several generations of characters and blues singers as well as train workers, she extends personal stories into social ones. As the train travels from Chicago to New Orleans, characters listen to a radio broadcast of the prizefight between white boxer James Braddock and black champion Joe Louis. The train journey becomes mythic; it transcends African-American specificity as well as personal stories by asking us to imagine all journeys of hope and aspiration, all struggles to overcome prejudice and achieve dignity.

SUGGESTIONS FOR THE DAY:

Reflect on how you might give at least one theme personal, social, and universal implications.

Until tomorrow,
Linda

HOMEWORK FOR THE WEEK

Finish the play by weaving together and tying off threads of plot points and themes, saving the most important character decisions and revelations for last.

DAY 86

"O! What a war of looks was then between them."
—WILLIAM SHAKESPEARE, "Venus and Adonis"

TURN OFF THE SOUND

Hi Writers,

As you shape the ending, watch the play unfold from the Beginning without listening to what characters are saying. Pay attention to the flow of images as if your play were a movie. As one beat, unit or scene shifts into another, what is the stage image and how is it "telling" us your story, your ideas? You might discover you've relied too much on words and haven't given your characters enough opportunities to show feelings and reactions. You also might discover you aren't giving the audience enough theatrical elements for transitions and sheer entertainment.

A play usually gives more importance to language than you'll find in movies, but the principles of visual story-telling are similar. Film and television evolved from live theatre. You can become so focused on dialogue and monologues that you forget your play's visual life. The audience won't, however. By "watching" your play unit by unit you can "track" characters' changes, their alignments and re-alignments with and against one another. This should help you weave and tie threads together as you write through climax and conclusion.

Watching with the sound off also helps you pay attention to subtext, the play's "other" action, which creates potential for a compelling visual performance at odds with the spoken text. How do George and Martha watch one another in *Who's Afraid of Virginia Woolf*? They can't have the same way of looking at each other or turning away through the whole play—each visual scene of the two of them should express what words can't about the progression of their relationship. Ophelia encounters Hamlet when, at her father's insistence, she seeks to return letters he had written her. Hamlet wears his "antic" mask, pretending to be crazed by his father's death. While in the text she says she long has longed to return these items and he responds to her harshly, is that truly what is happening between them? Is she pretending as well as Hamlet, behaving the way her father (hidden and listening) wishes while secretly harboring feelings at odds with what she is saying? What might we see in the way the lovers look at one another?

SUGGESTIONS FOR THE DAY:

1. Review your draft's visual life for action, musicality, character turns, audience clarity, movement, gestures, and juxtapositions that keep the play varied and logical. What does the beginning of each scene look like? How do characters enter and/or begin interacting?
2. How have you employed theatrical elements such as objects, light, scene changes, entrances, and exits to show the play moment by moment?
3. Study key plot points such as the point of attack. If an audience had only those key moments to follow like cartoon panels, would they see the progression of your drama?

Until tomorrow,
Linda

DAY 87

"All art is autobiographical—the pearl is the oyster's autobiography.

—FEDERICO FELLINI

KNOW THYSELF

Hi Writers,

"Knowing" ourselves is like trying to hold a river with our hands. And yet we persist. The better we know ourselves, our imaginations and habits, the better we can write. We hope we can become better people as well, more capable of recognizing the inner lives of those around us and responding to others, especially to the people we love. Writing is a form of self-expression, but plays should communicate with others and not just satisfy our personal needs. It is of little use to us or our audiences if we don't examine the ways in which we express ourselves as well as the ways in which we avoid expression. There is much to plumb from writing one play.

Identify possibilities you might have resisted while putting these characters into dramatic conflict. Are they inhibited by your inhibitions, your avoidance of conflict? Are you controlling them too much through a personal inclination to retain control or through a fear of loss of control? Perhaps your characters fly off the handle without the ability to compromise or listen to one another—is this behavior an issue for you? At what junctures in the process of storytelling do you encounter "blocks"? For Pablo Picasso his art was "a way of seizing the power by giving form to our terrors as well as our desires."

Finding our own "blind spots" is a lifelong struggle that an artistic life demands we join. As Fellini reminds us, all that we've experienced in life, the damage and the good we've done, all that's been done to us, is grit for creating pearls. Whether in art or in personal relationships, the better we understand the nature of our grit—the better the pearls. "Writing a poem is discovering," according to poet Robert Frost. Writing becomes not just a way of knowing ourselves, but also of expanding, revising, and ideally improving ourselves. The more you write courageously from self-awareness the better you can inspire others to be bold within their selves.

SUGGESTIONS FOR THE DAY:

1. What aspects of you are in these characters you have placed into conflict? Where are "you" in what excites them, what disgusts them, what puzzles and amazes? What do you know personally of their angers and fears, impulses, secrets, defenses and deflections?
2. Identify possibilities you might have resisted while creating dramatic conflict.
3. Reflect on what you've learned about yourself and your process as you bring this first draft to an end and before you attempt revision.

Until tomorrow,
Linda

DAY 88

"[A] poem . . . begins in delight and ends in wisdom
. . . in a clarification of life—not necessarily a great
clarification, such as sects and cults are founded on, but
in a momentary stay against confusion."
                                            —ROBERT FROST

HOW DO WE END?

Hi Writers,

In these 90 Days you have focused on driving your characters and their action through a scenario of plot points to a conclusion. Dramatic intrusions, especially the inciting incident, have forced inevitable clashes and consequences that led to crisis and climax. Your characters and audience have been given the opportunity to learn, feel, and possibly change as a result of this dramatic journey. Your resolution focuses on the most important lessons, emotions and changes. Remain open to discovery as your characters make the decisions and turnings they must coming from climax into conclusion. If you're not sure how to complete the play, write your alternative conclusions and don't decide until you rewrite which one will be "the one."

The resolution can slowly fade as in *The Cherry Orchard* when aged servant Fiers dies forgotten in the house as the first ax falls on a cherry tree. It's as if the themes have overtaken the play and characters fade into mist. Or, the resolution can come abruptly, as when Agnes and Peter set their motel room on fire in *Bug*.

You might devise an *epilogue*, an additional beat that completes the action thematically. For the Greeks an epilogue was an exit by a chorus, while in classical theatre it transformed into a direct address to the audience. Now you see it in the final moment of *August: Osage County*, in which Vi sings while the maid chants, each giving a version of life's ending. It's in Mama's final remarks in *'night, Mother* and the image of the son writing his suicide note in *Clybourne Park*.

Don't expect to create a perfect play. Not only is perfection impossible, but often it's the idiosyncrasies of your personality, your style, that make the play more resonant and distinctive. As Leonard Cohen sings, "There is a crack in everything. That's how the light gets through." If you haven't been able to tie up all the plot and theme threads by now, note which ones are dangling and wait until your rewrites to either incorporate or edit them.

SUGGESTIONS FOR THE DAY:

1. Review past exercises and exercises at the back of this book for creating climax and resolution.
2. Experiment with a variety of resolutions to discover which one or ones tie up the threads and satisfy you aesthetically and emotionally.
3. What are the most important lessons, emotions and changes or lack of changes in your play and how does your conclusion focus on those?

Until tomorrow,
Linda

DAY 89

"As we develop a storyline I always ask, what new information have we learned in this scene? How is the story moving forward? How are the stories talking to each other? How is this building? How is the end better than the beginning? Is the end even in the beginning?
—**ROBERT CARLOCK,** *30 Rock*

AN END

Hi Writers,

You are creating the final beats of your play. As you bring your play to an end, you are also bringing a story of your own to an end—the story of how you wrote this play. Through the process you probably learned something new about yourself and others. I hope you find this has enriched you. If you're still struggling with the resolution, today's exercises should help.

How will you know when you have finished your work on the play? The first step is to reach the point where you can't think of more ways to improve it and need to hear actors read it. You will revise after that and ready the draft for production. You might need to revise further after production.

At some point only you can decide that you have completed what you alone can do for this play. Enjoy all the time between now and then. Non-fiction writer John McPhee writes, "People often ask how I know when I'm done—not just when I've come to the end, but in all the drafts and revisions and substitutions of one word for another how do I know there is no more to do? When am I done? I just know. I'm lucky that way. What I know is that I can't do any better; someone else might do better, but that's all I can do; so I call it done."

SUGGESTIONS FOR THE DAY:

1. Review the logline/action statement you used earlier. Has that changed? If so, write a new one.
2. Write about at least one thing you hope people will want to talk about after they've seen your play.
3. Observe how your play is like and yet not like conventional genres and styles.
4. Note issues you'll need to address in a rewrite—everything from plot questions to character inconsistencies.
5. Describe the shape of your play from beginning to end.

Until tomorrow,
Linda

DAY 90

"Nobody tells this to people who are beginners, I wish someone told me. All of us who do creative work, we get into it because we have good taste. But there is this gap. For the first couple years you make stuff, it's just not that good. . . . A lot of people never get past this phase, they quit. Most people I know who do interesting, creative work went through years of this. We know our work doesn't have this special thing that we want it to have. We all go through this. And if you are just starting out or you are still in this phase, you gotta know it's normal and the most important thing you can do is a lot of work."

—**IRA GLASS**

LEARNING FROM OTHER WRITERS

Hi Writers,

Congratulations! Look back at where you began and celebrate your accomplishments in only three months. You should feel amazed and gratified by the characters who have invaded your life, the stories they've enacted for you to record, and the play with words you invented on your own. Print all you've done into a hard copy, save everything on your computer and flash drive or other backup device. Email the play to yourself so you can access it no matter what. Soon you will work on the play once more. Enjoy bringing one draft to conclusion, shifting perspectives, and then beginning again to revise your play with new ideas. However, put the play aside after you finish it today to cleanse the palate.

Because a playwright is a craftsperson who understands the mechanics of drama, I encourage you to make detailed analyses of plays' inner workings. The architecture of plays teaches you about characters, language, structure, theatricality and theme. While it's valuable to understand a play in its historical context as well as its genre and style, I have deliberately taken another approach in these letters. Study points of attack, monologues, point/counterpoint dialogue, multiple storylines and other architectural aspects of plays without pigeonholing them by era or genre. Look closely at the beginning of *Hamlet* and then the beginning of *August: Osage County* and *Bug.*

Combine readings in the classics with immersion in the best of contemporary drama. The classics have withstood time in part because they are so well constructed and so dense figuratively and thematically that they seem to activate audience's feelings across centuries and cultures. Aeschylus, Sophocles and Euripides built on the work of predecessors and peers to create some of the most enduringly powerful plays ever imagined. They strike thematic chords at the personal, social and universal levels while entertaining with extraordinary characters and vivid language. The standard translations are by David Grene and Richmond Lattimore or by Edith Hamilton. Look for contemporary translations as well, especially those by Anne Carson.

From the silliest farces to the most thoughtful works Moliere covered human behavior in ways both brilliantly entertaining and uniquely insightful. If you can read French, study how Racine uses every facet of language to create tone and build emotional intensity. Similarly, if you read Spanish, observe how the variety of meters and rhyme schemes in Lope de Vega's *Fuente Ovejuna* underscore subtext and create musical juxtapositions. Translations from French by Richard Wilbur and from Spanish by Edward Hall can inspire you as well because the translators are dramatic poets. William Shakespeare has left us an astonishing banquet of dramatic ideas. By all means read the most famous tragedies and comedies, but explore the lesser known works for plot inventions, themes and extraordinary language play.

Investigate the major works of the early modern writers such as Anton Chekhov and Henrik Ibsen, Bernard Shaw, the Irish writers and Eugene O'Neill, then Lorraine Hansberry, Lillian Hellman, Clifford Odets, Samuel Beckett— now the list becomes so long and varied that you should make your own choices based on styles and voices that intrigue you. British and American writers in the 1960s and 70s broke open forms and created new flights of language and fancy: see Sam Shepard, David Hare, Harold Pinter, Caryl Churchill. For unusual approaches to structuring plays, look at the work of Adrienne Kennedy, Maria Irene Fornes, ntozake shange, Charles Mee, Anna Deveare Smith, Tony Kushner, Annie Baker, John Guare. Read the Pulitzer and Tony award-winning plays of the past decade. Mix up your menu with plays by men and women and plays by writers from a broad range of ages and cultures.

SUGGESTIONS FOR THE DAY:

1. Practice asking questions of yourself, your work, and dramatic creations by other writers.
2. Dissect the architecture of plays to further your command of craft.
3. Keep writing new work, sending it out, learning from criticism you're receiving and the honest internal editor you're developing. Don't dwell on any play making the rounds of theatres and contests—focus on what you're writing in the present. The arrow flies forward.

Best wishes to you and the play,
Linda

WEEK 13: THOUGHTS AND REMINDERS

- Examine the ways a theme has impact in personal, social, and universal ways.

- Watch your play with the sound off, beat by beat, to review for action, theatricality, musicality, character turns, audience clarity, movement, gestures, and juxtapositions that keep the play's visual life varied, suggestive and logical.

- Reflect on what you've learned about yourself and your process as you bring this first draft to an end.

- Enjoy completing your play. Step away from it for self-reflection before plunging in again with fresh vision.

- Make detailed analyses of many plays' inner workings to study the craft of wrighting.

- Rewriting is your opportunity to improve and nurture both what you have written and your knowledge of craft.

rewriting
readings
submission
production

REWRITING

*"Re-vision—the act of looking back, of seeing with fresh
eyes, of entering an old text from a new critical direction."*
—ADRIENNE RICH

Rewriting is work and play, addition and subtraction: You add to make the play more dimensional, clear, logical, exciting, surprising. You subtract like a sculptor, cutting away what isn't needed or appropriate to the cleanest, clearest form. Don't become discouraged about your play as you identify places that don't work the way you think they should. Step by step, reviewing the principles, you'll improve the play and your knowledge of craft.

Revise on a printed copy of the script so you can pencil notes in the margins and experiment with changes.

Read your play all the way through to yourself out loud, alone. Without breaking the flow, note the points you might "fix." Read this way several times until you feel you grasp the rhythms and patterns of the whole play and have identified sections that need revision. Make notes separately in your play journal after each read-through. Note what you might need to do to clarify plot logic and character spine (reading backwards and then forwards, reviewing notes you made page by page).

Next read each character through out loud to trace his/her role in the action. Read for consistency, plausibility, and variety in each character's behavior and language.

Where does the theme appear/disappear? Note inconsistencies, redundancies.

Look for every opportunity to add spice, cut to the chase, shape musically.

Pay attention to repetitive vocabulary, redundancies, overstated themes.

Make sure everything said and done is necessary and interesting.
Review and apply lessons from the daily letters.
Chart individual sections and the entire action.

READINGS

Some writers find it helpful to hear their work read aloud by actors while it's being revised. However, your script should be as "finished" as possible before you open it to public response. A reader should be someone familiar with theatre and play readings, someone who knows how to respond to a writer's work, especially early drafts. Find good actors who are familiar with new plays. Friends who aren't good actors can make a mess of things. Actors who are used to the classics might not know how to respond to a work in progress.

Give each actor his/her separate copy of the play. Make sure the actors read through the play on their own beforehand so they can give a thoughtful reading rather than a "cold" one. You'll want them to pay attention to the music of the play as well as character development.

Consider letting your *first reading* be for you only with no "audience" other than the readers. You might catch problems you don't want to put before anyone else. Also, you can see if the actors you've chosen can do justice to your script, in case you need to replace any for future readings. The first reading should be primarily for you to hear the play. Have readers sit around a table or in a similar configuration so they can see one another as they read. You or someone else should read stage directions.

Provide food and drink for your readers and for anyone who takes the time to attend. Provide them with paper and pens or pencils for commentary. Thank them for their generosity both before and after the reading.

Make the *rules of a reading* clear to everyone beforehand. Do you want anyone to comment or is this just for you? If you want comments, and especially if you've invited others to listen, it still should conform to what you need. Tell people where you are in your process. Is it an early draft? Set up ahead of time where you want comments to focus. You'll learn more from specific comments than from general reactions.

Here are *questions* that should prove useful for them to answer: Are the characters true to the style and genre? Are they plausible within your play's style, within the rules of your game? Did anything in the dialogue seem clunky? Was the plot logical? If not, at which point(s)? (Note—it might be that the plot is logical and they just didn't listen well or couldn't imagine the play in production well enough to be discerning.)

People can be encouraged to jot down a word or two to help them remember points to make after the end of the play. However, they shouldn't stop paying attention to write comments. You want actors and audience to stay in the flow of the play. If they lose sight of the Big Picture while they're writing comments they won't be very useful to you.

At the end of the reading, give people time to gather their thoughts and jot comments they feel would benefit you. You might want only written comments instead of group discussion.

Guide the *discussion afterwards* rather than just opening up for comments. It can help to have a trusted moderator other than you. Make it clear that you will appreciate responses that are specific and descriptive. You don't need for people to be prescriptive, to start re-writing the play for you. If anyone starts doing that, stop them as politely as possible. Don't have expectations about how people will respond. Remain open to whatever you hear and know that only you can make sense of the responses. You are there to learn. Listen, don't argue. Ask for clarification if you don't understand a comment. Treat this like an experiment. Remain objective with your ego and pride in check. Don't be surprised if you hear conflicting opinions—what worked well for one person might puzzle another. Try to get to the heart of those conflicts later for yourself.

Rewrite further based on what you learn from readings.

SUBMISSION

Only when you believe the play is finished should you copyright and/or register it.

Copyright. Although you own the copyright to the play without registering it, put it in a sealed envelope, write your name across the seal before mailing it and then don't open the envelope when it returns in the mail, to prove when that draft was completed.

Registration. Register the final draft with the Library of Congress or the Writers Guild. That isn't necessary, but if it gives you comfort you can find information online about how to do that.

When you believe the play is ready for production, use *Writers Digest* (the magazine and the annual publication) and *American Theatre* magazine to study what agents, theatres, contests and festivals want before you submit to them. Search "playwriting contests" online but do your best to research an organization before sending your work there. It's best to avoid agents or contests that charge a fee.

Work with theatres near you that develop and produce new work. Most regional theatres want to encourage local talent. Volunteer for a theatre you think might be appropriate for your play; the staff there probably will read and critique the play for you in return.

Don't let rejection discourage you. The prize-winning play *Wit* was rejected by theatres all over the country before finally finding production. However, if you receive a dozen or more rejections you might revisit the play for further rewriting.

PRODUCTION

If you have an opportunity for production of your play outside of an academic setting, have a lawyer or agent represent you in creating a contract with the producer. Even if no money is exchanged, you should be careful to control your rights.

Don't let just anyone direct and/or produce your play solely because you want to see it. A dreadful production by people who don't understand it can set you back. Research the production histories of anyone interested in working with you.

In rehearsal, respect the production team and let the director do his/her job. Don't talk with a dramaturge, actors or designers unless the director asks you to do so. You can confuse everyone and sabotage the production.

Be prepared to rewrite in rehearsal.

additional exercises

Writing exercises are games you play with your imagination, puzzles you solve, creative gymnastics that enliven your memories and fantasies. Exercises can help you ease into and out of your day's work on a play, or they can fill your writing time today and prepare you for tomorrow's work. They are no substitute for your play, but they might give you insights you won't have otherwise. My goal is to help you merge a flowing imagination with attention to a play's architecture.

The following exercises are organized by category (Character, Language and so forth); for each category there is an index to exercises in the daily letters. You will find many overlaps. For example, an exercise that targets Language will also help you develop Character. Most exercises address Character and Structure in some way. These are additions to the exercises in your daily letters. Some are designed to address work on a play specifically while others are intended to be useful to your writing in general. Almost all can be adapted from the specific to the general and vice versa, and almost all can be used in a writers group or classroom. Most of the exercises should help you write novels, short stories, screenplays and teleplays as well.

CHARACTER

1. Scene by scene, describe how your character is being challenged, how s/he is responding.
2. What flaws do we see in each character? Does the character see them?
3. What do your characters know, or think they know, about their situation, choices and obstacles? What changes and why as the play progresses?
4. Have each character write a letter telling the others what they really think/want to say/wish. Have them explain what they are afraid to say and why. If it is in character for him/her to express himself/herself badly, use that in the letter.
5. Are your characters' memories reliable? Does the audience know one way or the other?
6. For each character: How do they feel about each other? What do they know about each other? How do women in your play feel about men, and vice versa?
7. At the beginning of each scene, where is each character (including those offstage)? Why? Doing what? Why does each character enter? Why does each one leave?
8. What effect do entrances and exits have on your story? On other characters?
9. Defend the necessity of each character in terms of action and theme. Could the play work without that character?
10. For each character: What are his/her physical habits?
11. For each character: What is his/her physical appearance? Is s/he slovenly? Why?
12. For each character: What music does s/he prefer? Books? Films? TV?
13. For each character: What is his/her background (i.e., social class, financial class, family, ethnicity, education, geography, culture, religion, politics)?

14. Are your characters good listeners? Do they interrupt? Do they reveal their feelings as they listen? Do they use silence as a weapon? Do they guard their thoughts with silence?

15. Who claims the center or primary place in a relationship? Do the others realize it? How do others react? Is there a struggle for that position? What happens if that person is dislodged from the center?

16. Does one character silence others? When? How? Is s/he aware s/he does that? How do people react to that?

17. What is each character's belief system with regard to right and wrong, God?

18. Does anyone "erase" him/herself in the presence of others? How? Is s/he aware of that? Are others? How do people react to that?

19. How do we learn about each character from what others say about him/her?

20. How does each character reflect, enhance, and/or help bring into focus the main character (protagonist) as well as the spine of action and theme?

21. Your characters are on the verge of change, whether they know it or not. For each character, describe that edge, that verge. Does the character know it? Why yes or no? What are his/her feelings about it? What is s/he doing to fight it or make it happen? Does s/he think something entirely different is about to happen?

22. Imagine each character as an animal. How does s/he cross the stage? Behave with others? Does s/he slink, slither, fly, lumber, skitter, charge?

23. Read obituaries. Write obituaries for each of your characters. Return to these as you proceed with your play to see if you need to change their life stories.

24. How does each character sign his/her name?

25. If your character could be anyplace else, doing anything else, what would it be?

26. Have your characters recount their dreams (literal and figurative).

27. If each character were a musical instrument, what kind would s/he be? What kind of music would s/he play?

28. Construct dialogue between or among characters who misunderstand what each is saying.

29. Do your characters play anything together, like charades, cards, golf? Can you use that to have them argue? Flirt? Belittle?

30. Two of your characters are in a location in your play (living room, forest, etc.). They hear something offstage. Write their reactions to it.

31. How are your characters like/unlike character "types" (innocent maiden, warrior hero, braggart soldier, lecherous old man, noble prince, meddling neighbor, etc.)?

32. For any character whose home is different from what we see onstage—describe it.

33. Have each character finish this statement. Elaborate on why they say what they do.
    "What I look forward to most each day is . . ."
    "What I dread most each day is . . ."

34. Play with similes to describe your characters. Use terms that aren't human to illustrate their appearance and behavior and make them more concrete for you. (Ex.: M. Beauchamps is like a massive rotting fig, a boulder blocking the road, a carcass only a fly could love; Joseph is like a wraith, a cypress shedding bark.)

35. At the moment of crisis in your play, what is the main character trying to do? What's going wrong? What does s/he need to see and do differently?

36. What is the audience's stake in the outcome of your characters' decisions?

37. What is the audience relationship to your main character from beginning to end? How do we get "in" to that character; that is, how does the play provide a "door" for empathy?

38. How do lying and/or truth telling serve your drama?

39. What do your main characters agree on? Why?

40. What does Character A wish Character B would say to him/her? (write a monologue)
    Reverse that for Character B's wish.

41. What are the key features in each of your secondary characters? Annoying? Mysterious?

42. What happens to your main characters after the play ends? Imagine each character in the future writing to him/herself—say ten years from now—about this time, what s/he learned, what changed, what

remained unclear.

Find additional character exercises in these daily letters: 3, 4, 5, 6, 7, 8, 9, 10, 11, 12, 13, 14, 15, 16, 18, 19, 25, 32, 34, 35, 36, 39, 50, 51, 53, 54, 55, 56, 57, 58, 60, 61, 62, 63, 64, 66, 70, 71, 72, 75, 84, 87.

LANGUAGE

1. Spend time where people like your characters gather—listen to them, write snippets of what you hear. Collect rhythms, patterns, vocabulary. Figure out what's interesting and what isn't, reflect on why you've made those decisions.
2. What is each character's favorite expressions?
3. Read plays, poetry, and novels that are something like the 'diction" you have in mind.
4. Listen to songs that are like your diction.
5. Create dialogue in which your characters do not argue logically with one another.
6. Imagine your characters singing their dialogue. You might discover awkward or needlessly repetitive phrasing this way.
7. List five or more of your favorite words. Put two of your characters in dialogue using them. Have a character deliver a monologue using them.
8. Throw open the dictionary to three words. Have one of your characters use these words in a monologue. Or, have characters use them in dialogue.
9. One character says, "Bright like," and another finishes the simile. Does the first like it, or do they argue over the choice?
10. Do the above exercise with metaphors, symbols, onomatopoeia.
11. How does each character's way of speaking illustrate personality, confidence, education, economic class, background, etc.? Does that change as the character changes?
12. As you read your play aloud, are there too many of the same sounds? The same cadences? Do all characters sound the same? Are the sounds percussive, smooth, lilting? Do they contrast? Are there

variations in volume? Do the sounds suit the scene and the play?

13. For each character, what is his/her "characteristic" vocabulary, diction, phrases (i.e, describe and give examples for each character's speech behavior)? For example: "Don't waste my time," "I'll make it worth your while," "Show me," "What do you want?," "Make me an offer," "Get to the point."

14. Create a poem or song as one or more of your characters (it can be silly).

15. Write a stream of consciousness monologue for a main character when the play reaches crisis beginning with "I'm confused, uncertain about what direction to take because . . ."

    Now bring in another significant character to counter, question or support that monologue in a monologue of his/her own.

    Set the two into dialogue over reactions to those two monologues. Do their "voices" remain separate and consistent?

16. Have each character tell at least one lie about him/herself.

Find additional language exercises in these daily letters: 4, 5, 9, 11, 32, 39, 46, 50, 51, 61, 63, 66, 73, 74, 84

GENERAL LANGUAGE EXERCISES

1. To explore subtext, pick anything for a text—the Declaration of Independence or a song like "This Old Man." Say or sing it as if you're looking at another person and thinking something completely different (fear, loathing, attraction, suspicion). Try numerous subtexts with the same text.

2. What are some of today's shared metaphors/similes that work for you the way hunting and rowing did for the Greeks and gardens did for Shakespeare? Think of your activities—might a large number of people have them in common? Sports? Gardening? Commuting? Cooking?

3. Write a simple sentence. Consider how many different ways it can be delivered depending on the character, intention, and context. Ex.: "I told you I'll fix it tomorrow."

Now write a simple dialogue exchange with the same exploration of variations. Example:

"Where are you going?"

"No place special."

4. Imagine a character. Let the following statements be the beginning of a monologue by that character: "I could have stopped her anytime I wanted. I don't know why I didn't."

"First it was 'yes.' Then it was 'no.'"

"I had no idea you felt that way."

Create similar statements for yourself as prompts.

5. What language do you most enjoy—in novels, songs, plays? Do you recall when you first really listened to words? What were they? Why do you think they appealed to you?

6. From the story of the Three Little Pigs, choose a pig or the wolf.

Write two or three different monologues for that same character, changing character "voice." Can you change the voice but keep the same character, or does the character change significantly depending on the voice?

PROCESS

1. Which aspect(s) of yourself is/are writing this play (i.e., your romantic self, your political self)?

2. As you're collecting and planning—ask if this is mostly a play of ideas? A romp? A comedy of manners? A mystery? A slice of life (whose life, what kind of life)? A romance? A tragedy with lessons learned? A dramedy with lessons learned?

3. What does your primary theme mean for you personally? How have you wrestled with this, what questions do you have, what uncomfortable memories, mistakes?

4. What about your play touches on your most deeply emotional experiences?

5. August Wilson was inspired by the blues—the music works as a structural motif but also as the ethos of his characters, their history, their struggles, his themes. Do you have a musical or visual reference

that inspires and guides you in this way?

6. When you've identified primary plot points, explore what you know and believe personally in relation to the conflicts, dissonance, challenges and alliances. Reflect on your observations and personal experiences, your treatment of others, what coping mechanisms you've devised to deal with these, what you watch others doing.

7. Review other stories, plays, films you know with themes and characters (not just plot points or style) similar to yours. How might those help you refine your choices?

8. What about your idea makes you uncomfortable?

9. When you're ready to begin—write a short summary of your play— like you might find in a newspaper review (read some). Don't worry if you can't do it perfectly, and feel free to write several versions, employing different endings. Identify where you draw a blank. Every week return to this summary and see what you can fill in, what must change.

10. Even if you think you know what your story is and what your play is about, take time to play "what if?" How many other directions could it take?

11. At the end of each unit, how have your feelings about writing the play changed or remained the same? Why? Are your feelings getting in the way of your writing or nourishing your imagination?

12. If your play were a painting, a song, symphony, or a film what aspects of it would be present in that other art form? How would it be different?

13. Either before you write a scene or after, or both: narrate action by action, topic by topic, what you think must happen. Who is driving the action and why? Who is thwarting whom, and why? What significant information is being given the audience and why at this time? What will be the climax of this scene? Is this a turning point? Practice being as focused and specific as possible as you work. This plan might change entirely as soon as you begin the scene. Don't fight that. Let the scene that wants to emerge take shape. Then look back at your initial plan and consider which of those ideas might belong in another scene or in a rewrite.

14. As you finish a scene or episode, ask what in that scene is arousing

curiosity? What is satisfying curiosity?

15. Imagine an overture for your play. What would it sound like and how would it set up your play in terms of tone, pace, theme, style, genre?

16. When you finish the first draft, what have you learned regarding your main themes that you didn't know when you began?

17. When you finish the first draft, imagine the color palette for the play. See how that changes as the action flows.

18. What are your strengths as a writer? How might we see this in your play? (i.e., what's best about your play?)

Find additional process exercises in these daily letters: 1, 13, 15, 21, 22, 26, 28, 29, 30, 31, 33, 37, 38, 42, 44, 48, 49, 52, 54, 59, 67, 79, 82, 83, 86, 87, 89, 90.

GENERAL PROCESS EXERCISES

1. Go to museums. Spend time in the company of art that resonates for you, especially art that is somehow emotionally and stylistically related to your play.

2. Take one story—comic, dramatic, musical theatre—and explore how changing genres and styles might change a story.

3. To help get into writing and aid focus on specifics, tell stories in response to this prompt: Your first (or the first you can remember): pet, friend, teacher, home, fear, music, or any other topics as they come to you.

4. What are some memorable moments in theatre for you (good or bad or both) and why are they memorable? What does this suggest to you as a writer?

5. What is a play to you? Imitation of an action? An illusion? Mirror held to nature? Blueprint for performance? Diversion? Polemic? Proverb writ large? Or is it something concrete in and of itself? Some or all of these?

6. What circumstances help you write best? What time of day? Listening to music? Total solitude or laptop at the coffee shop? How many hours a day?

7. From *Who's Afraid of Virginia Woolf?* to *Angels in America*, observe the aspects of all sorts of structures and writing choices that delight you. Try to describe what "works."

8. What aspects of human nature completely baffle you? Why?

9. What kind of learner are you? Do you think associatively and then pull everything together (that's me)? Do you think in a linear process? Do you make lists (I do)? Do you need visuals, graphs, charts?

10. Do you resist planning a play? Why? How does that help or hinder?

11. Do you procrastinate? Or are you a disciplined writer?

12. What makes you weep? Angry? Fearful? Joyful? And, why?

13. Write about your personal emotional landscape so you can employ it in your writing. The life you put onstage should come from your inner spirit, the depths of your emotional experience, even if it's a rollicking comedy.

14. What kind of writing do you most like to read?

15. Write stream-of-consciousness on each of the following topics:
    • Think of three objects. Write a story (or playlet) utilizing them.
    • Three strangers are on an island. Who? Why? What are they doing? Something strange washes up on shore.
    • Create a silly poem/song as one of your characters.
    • You begin to cross a bridge but are stopped by a troll.

16. If you're feeling "blocked" or dull-witted: Create in another medium. Paint, garden, cook, sing, dance, sketch, take photographs, play an instrument.

17. Loglines/Action statements: Describe the heart (core) of the action of familiar stories, myths.

18. Select one or more characters; they can be from your play or not. Imagine her/him or them in a randomly selected image. Now imagine what story might have them in this image. Repeat this exercise several times with the same characters—finding different images and different stories.

STRUCTURE

1. List five things that should happen in your play (plot points) without worrying about the order. Try variations on the order. How does each arrangement affect the overall story?

2. Does your story have elements of a familiar myth or story (for example, Cinderella, Oedipus, Odysseus)? What are the similarities and differences? How might you take advantage of the similarities? How should you play against audience expectation?

3. Before tackling point of attack and scenario, write out the full story in a linear narrative (like a short story) that identifies each plot point in linear order. Note which plot points can or even should be left off stage and which are part of the past (sometimes called the "backstory").

4. Divide your rough scenario for the Middle into a beginning, middle, and end. Consider each as an episode. List one or more key plot points that should occur in each third without worrying about scenario order. What fills or provides transitions between the episodes?

5. After you've outlined your scenario, read it backwards. Are there problems in the logic?

6. If your scenario is a series of songs, what kind of music is each scene? Think of the Greek "ethos." What tone, rhythm and stimulus are you providing with each one? Salsa, punk, love ballad, Puccini opera, heavy metal?

7. Imagine your play as a cartoon of approximately five to seven panels, each of which captures key moments. What would those moments be?

8. Write an epilogue.

9. Imagine how each character would wrap up the conclusion and meaning of your play.

10. When you finish the first draft: Study the beginning 10-15 pages for how they set up the play. Now look at the final 10-15 pages to see if that set up was fulfilled.

11. Jot ideas for a preface for your play—sentence fragments are fine. What is its historical setting / literal place (city, even neighborhood)? What is happening socially in this time period that might resonate with your play (your characters, their struggles, your themes)? It can

be helpful to do this exercise before you revise.

Find additional structure exercises in these daily letters: 2, 3, 4, 9, 10, 15, 17, 18, 20, 21, 22, 23, 26, 27, 28, 30, 31, 34, 36, 40, 41, 42, 43, 44, 45, 47, 48, 52, 54, 59, 62, 64, 65, 66, 68, 71, 72, 75, 76, 77, 78, 80, 81, 86, 88, 89.

GENERAL STRUCTURE EXERCISES

1. This exercise helps you examine how story, plot and scenario differ from one another. It also incorporates point of view. The Cinderella story begins with her birth, and then goes through mother's death to her being chosen by the Prince, and beyond. Think of the slice of the *story* we know conventionally as the *plot*. It begins after the father has died and she's the servant to a stepmother and stepsisters. We know the plot points of that, and we're familiar with the Disney scenario (the arrangement of those plot points), which includes scenes with birds and a fat cat. The point of view is Cinderella's—her suffering, her dreams and her success.

   • Imagine twists—a different point of view, tone, even with someone other than Cinderella as the main character if you wish. You can introduce characters and change the familiar ones.

   • What might the plot points be in each different telling of the Cinderella story? Outline the scenes you would select to fulfill that plot—in what order. Think of beats and details for the scenes.

   • Take one slice of this story and its plot—perhaps the scene at the ball. Can you create an engaging drama from that one slice? Can you invent new ways of thinking about it?

2. Try the above exercise with The Three Little Pigs and expand on it. Review the familiar story—three pigs and a wolf, each pig builds a different house to stave off the wolf (straw, wood, brick), only the brick house holds. Imagine the larger dramatic world (village, forest, other animals, humans, time setting) Select a slice or two from that for plot points.

   • Characters—is there a main character? What are the character relationships (allies, antagonists, family, strangers, etc.)? Can you invent alternate approaches to conventional characters (for example, one pig must build from straw because she's poor and no one will help her)?

- Decide point of attack.
- Inciting Incident—what sets the play in motion?
- Scenario—arrange plot points for what we'll actually see.
- What are the obstacles, complications, intrusions, etc., leading to crisis, climax, resolution?
- Consider genre and style alternatives.
- Consider various approaches to plot/scenario/character.
- What is the relationship of the play to an audience (direct address, narrator, fourth wall illusion)?
- How do they speak (Clockwork Orange, 19th century, hillbilly)? How do they vary from one another?
- What is the theatrical style (realistic, cartoon, operatic)?
- Might music be used? If so, how?
- Themes—what are lessons learned? Does each plot/scenario choice result in the same lesson?

3. Study how your favorite works of art are composed. Practice observing the underlying architecture of works of art, from sonnets to symphonies.
4. Study beginnings of plays, films, TV series, TV episodes. See how the first few minutes define much of the adventure ahead—not just in terms of plot/story/characters but style, pace, genre, time period, place, humor.
   - What are the inciting incidents? Where do they occur in the plot and/or in the scenario? Why are they placed there? What do they generate?
   - How does theatricality introduce the theme and other elements?
   - How does the beginning relate to the end? To the theme?
5. Begin with the basic stories, plots and scenarios of plays and movies everyone knows, and then play "what if?"
6. Here are prompts/setups for scene writing practice. (See how reactions create action.)
   - A locker room. A lone basketball player sits on a bench, apparently dejected. The coach enters from the back, sees the player, and halts

without saying anything. One of them speaks first—write their exchange.

- An apartment living room. Everything is in disarray, as if a bull ran through it. Someone enters from outside, carrying a suitcase, and stops to survey the wreckage. Write that person's reactions.
- An empty stage. Someone slowly pushes a broom across it. Someone else runs onstage from the other direction. Write their exchange.

7. Create a music set list that works like a scenario.

8. How is a play like a secret?

9. Practice writing in one sentence the core throughline (action statement/logline) of plays and films you like. Example from *Boy Gets Girl*: A writer who flees a dangerous stalker learns to claim her own true self and passion.

10. Study the beats in a contemporary play you like that is closely related to yours in genre and style. How do the beats begin and end? How do they "tie in" to one another? Can you see how some beats are transitional and others are topical?

11. Study the structure in music you like. Graph the progression of theme and variation, bridges, the rising and falling tension, crescendo and decrescendo, the minor chord/the major lift. Note the use of instruments and voices—contrasts, surprises, solos, complexity. If it's a song with a repeating chorus, does the chorus become needlessly repetitive? If not, how do the musicians play with it to sustain interest?

12. It has been said that there are only a few basic plots and structures, for example, "boy meets girl, boy loses girl, boy gets girl," or "overcoming tyranny." Think of as many familiar storylines as possible in five minutes. *Boy Gets Girl* plays "what if" with that familiar story. Play "what if" with one or more of the stories you've identified, up-ending the conventional with twists.

13. Analyze a contemporary play you like. Graph/chart the structure. Write down what you learn from doing this. Be your own Aristotle.

14. Consider how the same story can be rendered with differing scenarios in differing media (for example, Alice in Wonderland as a play, TV series).

15. Play structures are like: fireworks, an exciting athletic contest, a well

told story, a tightening noose, a ticking clock, a murder mystery, a heist, a still pond hit by a rainstorm. Describe how each of those is suited to a play's structure.

16. How might obstacles be the same as or different from complications? Do obstacles lead to complications? Can an obstacle or complication actually help the protagonist?

17. Some plays make fun of conventional storytelling and playwriting (for example, *The Skin of Our Teeth*, *The Real Inspector Hound*, *The Bald Soprano*, *Ubu Roi*). Study them to understand what they spoof.

THEATRICALITY

1. If you call for an actor to play multiple roles, explain why. How does that advance entertainment, theme, style, plot? How can the audience be clear and not confused by this device?

2. What might characters be doing in the beginning (and elsewhere in the play) that will give us the what-when-where-how-who-why information (exposition) without anyone's having to explicitly tell the audience?

3. You should see the play as you write it. If the action takes place in a living room, who decorated it? How does the décor reflect character? If it's an office, is it downscale or corporate? What is the color palette?

4. What theatrical elements signal style from the beginning of your play?

5. Imagine your scenes (sound off) with musical accompaniment, like a silent movie.

6. Listen to your scenes with your eyes closed. What if you can't understand the language?

   Other than the meaning in the words, is there musicality? Variation? Contrast?

Find additional theatricality exercises in these daily letters: 6, 8, 12, 24, 34, 38, 41, 71, 84, 86

GENERAL THEATRICALITY EXERCISES

You're in the audience of a theatre, and see a theatre/stage (perhaps the theatre where your play might take place). There's a pool of light on the stage. See a chair in the light.

Walk onto the stage and sit in the chair. Look out into the audience—it's too dim to make out faces. Sense the audience. What kind of people, how many, how are they dressed?

Become Character A, not yourself, perhaps a character in your play. No one you know.

Character A is holding an object. Look at it—write down what it is. Character A tells the audience a story about this object—a memory, a projection, a lie, anything.

Character B interrupts from offstage—"Stop!" Character B enters and approaches because of the object and the story (How? Who?). Again, not you, not anyone you know. B contradicts the story—directly or obliquely.

Now A stands and interrupts.

They engage in dialogue and movement spinning from the stories about the object, but there is no physical conflict.

THEME

1. Aristotle opined that a play should convey a "general truth." What does that mean to you?
2. What are the "general truths" in your play and how do you ask the audience to experience/think about them?
3. How are you showing themes theatrically? Justify each choice at each moment.

GENERAL THEME EXERCISES

Study a contemporary play you like.
- What is the main theme?
- What are minor themes?
- How do they interrelate (resonate with one another, support)?
- How are they carried out in the play (language, relationships, theatricality, other)?

GROUP THEME EXERCISE

Ask people to state the main themes of their plays. Invite others to tell their associations with those themes. Look for commonalities and universalities in those associations.

Find additional theme exercises in these daily letters: 13, 53, 56, 57, 76, 78, 85

index to
principles and terms

PREPARATION

Familiar situations and conflicts, adaptation, personal journal, play journal, drama, action, conflict, theatre, story, plot, scenario, structure of scenario, point of attack, protagonist, antagonist, language, theatricality, theme, style, tragedy, dramedy, comedy, melodrama, epic/Brechtian, fourth wall, direct address, stage directions, suspension of disbelief, stream-of-consciousness

CHARACTERS

(Day) 1:   inhabiting dramatic world
3:              importance of time, event, ticking clock
4:              inner tensions, contradictions, imbalances, what kind of character
5:              dissonance, relationships
6:              relationship to theatre space, relationship to audience
7:              his/her life story, past and future
9:              their pasts
10:            voice, monologue
11:            dualities, inner contradictions, public/private selves, masks
12:            differences, theatricality to illuminate character
14:            dialogue, interactions
15:            plot, plot points, main character/ protagonist, stakes
16:            plot points, main character/ protagonist
17:            plot points, supporting roles
18:            character as counterpoint
19:            antagonist(s), allies/confidant(s), doppelgangers, types, desires, conflict
24:            relationship with audience
25:            point of view, Boal technique

LANGUAGE

PROCESS

STRUCTURE

68:    dynamic substructure, Greek chorus/echoes and traces
       today, blending of chorus with action in crisis and climax,
       pace, meter, ethos, rhythm, mood, tone, transitions,
       considerations for nonlinear and non-realistic theatre
69:    crisis and climax, something happens beyond words,
       counterpoint, mediated images
70:    character roles in crisis
71:    turning points, crisis, climax, bridge, musicality
72:    envision End, varieties of endings and resolutions
76:    alternatives narrow in crisis and climax, suspend final
       outcome, keep alternative endings open for unpredictability
77:    role of the past in crisis and climax
78:    repetition, magic of three, making crisis and climax vivid
80:    varieties of endings, genre expectations, sense of closure,
       resolution, deus ex machina, epilogue
81:    shapes of plays (order/disorder/ resolution, thesis/antithesis/
       synthesis, ladder)
82:    closeups/medium shots/long shots, background/foreground,
       final image
86:    seeing the action with the sound off, flow of images
88:    resolution, epilogue
89   ending the draft

THEATRICALITY

(Day) 6:   theatre space, 4th wall (breaking or not), direct address,
            characters' relationship to theatre space
8:          introduction to theatricality (objects, setting, sound)
12:         illuminating character
25:         Boal technique
34:         entrances/exits
38:         multiple settings
41:         silence
58:         how characters move and speak, visual and musical variety
67:         overlapping/simultaneous speech
69:         mediated images

THEME

PART SIX

format
selected plays
selected bibliography
acknowledgments

FORMAT

If you don't use playwriting software, here are suggestions for formatting your script. These are designed to make your script appear professional, so the reader can shift from one kind of description to another and follow characters' speeches easily. See pages from Steve Totland's *You Are Here* in the Day 27 introduction to beats for examples of standard format.

Inanimate stage descriptions begin center page and run flush right, single-spaced. This includes information about when and where the scene takes place as well as what we see on the stage and the arrangement of playing spaces. If the description is lengthy, break it into blocks and single space between each block. For example, if this takes place in a living room you might describe furniture in one block and what we see on the walls in a separate block.

Animate stage directions begin about ten characters (two five character tabs) left of the inanimate descriptions and run flush right. These describe sound effects, light effects, and character movements. They, too, run flush right. You might break these into discrete blocks so a sound effect is on one line, then after a single space we read that a character enters.

Character names are capitalized and centered.

Character speeches run flush left to flush right.

If you must insert a direction into a character's speech, set it in brackets immediately before the speech it directs. Avoid this unless the direction is critical to telling the story and helping the audience understand the rules of the play. Example: [whispering] Has she left yet?

Describe what a character does in general terms appropriate to the story but not in every little detail. "She reads a magazine, occasionally turning the pages." Don't tell us every time she turns the page unless it's crucial to the action.

See Day 67 for formatting interruptions in characters' speeches and pauses as well as simultaneous conversations.

SELECTED PLAYS

(Plays referred to in *The 90-Day Play*)

Ackerman, Rob
    Call Me Waldo
Aeschylus
    The (An) Oresteia (Agamemnon, Orestes, The Eumenides)
Albee, Edward
    Who's Afraid of Virginia Woolf?
Baker, Annie
    Circle Mirror Transformation
    The Aliens
Beaumarchais, Pierre
    The Marriage of Figaro
Beckett, Samuel
    Happy Days
    Waiting for Godot
Brecht, Berthold
    The Good Person of Szechuan
Chekhov, Anton
    The Cherry Orchard
    Uncle Vanya
Churchill, Caryl
    Cloud 9
Cleage, Pearl
    Blues for an Alabama Sky
De Vega, Lope
    Life is a Dream (Vida es Sueno)
Donahue, John Clark
    Helen Deltz
Durrenmatt, Friedrich
    The Visit
Euripides
    The Bacchae
    Medea
    Trojan Women

Foote, Horton
    Vernon Early
Fornes, Maria Irene
    Fefu and Her Friends
Gilman, Rebecca
    Boy Gets Girl
    Spinning into Butter
Goldoni, Carlo
    A Servant of Two Masters
Gunderson, Lauren
    Emilie (La Marquise Du Chatelet Defends her Life Tonight)
Guare, John
    Landscape of the Body
Hagedorn, Jessica
    Dogeaters
Hall, Katori
    The Mountaintop
Handke, Peter
    Offending the Audience
    The Ride Across Lake Constance
Hansberry, Lorraine
    A Raisin in the Sun
Hwang, David Henry
    F.O.B.
    M. Butterfly
    The Dance and the Railroad
Ibsen, Henrik
    A Doll's House
    Hedda Gabler
Ionesco, Eugene
    The Bald Soprano
Jarry, Alfred
    Ubu Roi
Jent, Deanna
    Falling

Kalidasa
    The Sign of Shakuntala
Kaufman, George S. and Edna Ferber
    Dinner at Eight
Kennedy, Adrienne
    A Movie Star Has to Star in Black and White
    The Owl Answers
Kushner, Tony
    A Bright Room Called Day
    Angels in America
Letts, Tracy
    August: Osage County
    Bug
Logan, John
    Red
Machiavelli, Nicolo
    La Mandragola
Mamet, David
    American Buffalo
McDonagh, Martin
    The Pillowman
McPherson, Scott
    Marvin's Room
Marlowe, Christopher
    Tamberlaine
Mee, Chuck
    Investigation of Murder in El Salvador
Miller, Arthur
    Death of a Salesman
Moliere
    The Misanthrope
    Tartuffe
Nemeth, Sally
    Holy Days
    Mill Fire
Norman, Marsha
    'night, Mother

Sophocles
    Antigone
    Oedipus
    Philoctetes
Strindberg, August
    The Stronger
Totland, Steve
    You Are Here
Wagner, Jane
    Search for Signs of Intelligent Life in the Universe
West, Cheryl
    Pullman Porter Blues
Wilder, Thornton
    Our Town
Williams, Tennessee
    A Streetcar Named Desire
Willson, Meredith
    The Music Man
Wilson, August
    Joe Turner's Come and Gone
    Ma Rainey's Black Bottom
    The Piano Lesson

SELECTED BIBLIOGRAPHY

PERIODICALS AND ONLINE RESOURCES

American Theatre magazine for new American plays
TheatreForum for new international plays
Dramatics magazine
www.doollee.com for free online database of modern playwrights
    and theatre plays (since 1956) which have been written, adapted
    or translated into English since the production, includes agents,
    publishers, theatres
www.newplaysmap.org for where new plays are being produced in the
    United States
www.nnpn.org (National New Play Network) for alliance of non-profit
    theatres that champions the development, production and continued
    life of new plays
New resources come online frequently; search for them with key words
    such as "new plays" and "resources for playwrights."

BOOKS

Aristotle. *Poetics.*
Artaud, Antonin. *The Theatre and Its Double.*
Auerbach, Eric. *Mimesis.*
Ayckbourn, Alan. *The Crafty Art of Playmaking.*
Baker, George Pierce. *Dramatic Technique.*
Ball, David. *Backwards and Forwards. A Technical Manual for Reading
    Plays.*
Bentley, Eric. *The Playwright as Thinker.*
Breen, Robert. *Chamber Theatre.*
Brockett, Oscar G. and Franklin Hildy. *History of the Theatre.*
Brockett, Oscar G. with Robert Ball. *The Essential Theatre.*
Brockett, Oscar G. and Robert Findlay. *Century of Innovation. A History
    of European and American Theatre and Drama Since the Late
    Nineteenth Century.*

Burke, Kenneth. *A Grammar of Motives.*
   The Philosophy of Literary Form. Studies in Symbolic Action.
Brecht, Bertold and John Willett. *Brecht on Theatre: The Development of an Aesthetic.*
Brunello, Piero and Lena Lenchek, eds. *How to Write Like Chekhov.*
Carrillo, Elena, co-editor. *The Student's Guide to Playwriting Opportunities.*
Catron, Louis. *Writing, Producing and Selling Your Play.*
Chinoy, Helen Krich and Linda Walsh Jenkins, *Women in American Theatre. Third edition.*
Ciardi, John. *How Does a Poem Mean?*
Cocteau, Jean. *The Difficulty of Being.*
Cole, Toby. *Playwrights on Playwriting.*
Dikkers, Scott. *How to Write Funny.*
Dunne, Will. *The Dramatic Writer's Companion.*
Eagleton, Terry. *How to Read Literature.*
Esslin, Martin. *An Anatomy of Drama.*
Fenellosa, Ernest. *The Chinese Written Character as a Medium for Poetry.*
Fordin, Hugh. *Getting to Know Him* (biography of Oscar Hammerstein).
Galloway, Marian. *Constructing a Play.*
Geary, James. *I Is Another: The Secret Life of Metaphor and How It Shapes the Way We See the World.*
Grothe, Mardy. *I Never Metaphor I Didn't Like: A Comprehensive Compilation of History's Greatest Analogies, Metaphors, and Similes.*
Hatcher, Jeffrey. *The Art and Craft of Playwriting.*
Herrington, John, ed. *The Playwright's Muse.*
Ionesco, Eugene. *Notes and Counternotes.*
Jones, Catherine Ann. *The Way of Story.*
King, Stephen. *On Writing. A Memoir of the Craft.*
Kinzie, Mary. *A Poet's Guide to Poetry.*
Lakoff, George and Mark Johnson. *Metaphors We Live By.*
LaMotte, Anne. *Bird by Bird.*
Lawson, John Howard. *Theory and Technique of Playwriting.*
Libera, Anne and Second City Inc. *The Second City Almanac of Improvisation.*
McCabe, Terry. *Misdirecting the Play.*
Mee, Charles. Website: www.charlesmee.org

Olson, Elder. *Tragedy and the Theory of Drama.*

Parra, Angelo. *Playwriting for Dummies.*

Patchett, Ann. *The Getaway Car. A Practical Memoir About Writing and Life.*

Pettengill, Richard, Nicholas Cook, eds. *Taking It to the Bridge. Music as Performance.*

Pressfield, Steven. *The War of Art.*

Schechner, Richard. *Public Domain.*

Scruggs, Mary and Michael J. Gellman. *Process: An Improviser's Journey.*

Simon, Neil. *The Play Goes On: A Memoir.*

Smiley, Sam. *Playwrighting: The Structure of Action.*

Smith, Anna Deavere. *Talk to Me.*
    Letters to a Young Artist.

Spencer, Stuart. *The Playwright's Guidebook.*

States, Bert. *Dreaming and Storytelling.*

Sweet, Jeffrey. *The Dramatist's Toolkit, The Craft of the Working Playwright.*
    Solving Your Script: Tools and Techniques for the Playwright.

Van Itallie, Jean-Claude. *The Playwright's Workbook.*

Vorhaus, John. *The Comic Toolbox.*

Watt, Alan. *The 90-Day Novel.*
    The 90-Day Rewrite.
    The 90-Day Screenplay.

Williams, George G. *Creative Writing.*

Wood, David and Janet Grant. *Theater for Children: A Guide to Writing, Adapting, Directing and Acting.*

Writer's Digest

ACKNOWLEDGEMENTS

How I came to love studying plays and the ways they achieve meaning will always be something of a mystery to me. Certain people showed me the path, others opened doors, and many shared discoveries and talents in ways that have enriched me. I am very grateful to all who have marked this central trail through my life. My father, John Eugene Walsh (an excellent writer himself) showed me the best movies, told and read wonderful stories, introduced me to delightful poetry, and gave me the opportunity to perform in Fort Worth's remarkable Reeder's School when I was very young. While I majored in English at Rice University, John Ciardi's *How Does a Poem Mean?* hooked me on the architecture of literature. I earned my PhD in theatre at the University of Minnesota/Minneapolis. Through scholarships at both schools, teaching opportunities as a graduate student, and a Danforth Graduate Fellowship for Women, I was able to pursue these studies; I am very grateful for that inestimable support.

Minnesota's Twin Cities was an invigorating home for nine years. An emphasis on new plays began in 1967 when I read original scripts for Dr. Arthur Ballet's Office for Advanced Drama Research, which encouraged theatres globally to produce them before there was much in the way of nonprofit regional theatres. Jim Malcolm recommended me to Dr. Ballet, not realizing what effect that would have for my life's work. I am grateful to Joe Walsh and Fred Gaines for the opportunity to perform original sketches and one-acts with The Anyplace Theatre in1968. Working as an actress with writer-director John Clark Donahue in the Children's Theatre Company of the Minneapolis Art Institute (1968-1975) gave me an invaluable immersion in the new play process; every script was original and many were created during rehearsals. As Literary Manager, I edited two volumes of those scripts by Donahue and others, published in 1975 by the University of Minnesota Press (*The Cookie Jar and Other Plays, Five Plays from the Children's Theatre*). Those experiences led to my reading and critiquing scripts for the Tyrone Guthrie Theatre's second stage, Guthrie 2—thanks to David Ball.

I cannot summon sufficient gratitude for my students and colleagues at Northwestern University in Evanston, IL, where I was an assistant and then associate professor, 1976-89. I lectured in the history of theatre and dramatic literature and taught playwriting classes, but those remarkable people taught me far more than I could have given them. Thanks to funds from Northwestern alumna Agnes Nixon, we produced festivals of new work and developed plays throughout the year with readings and workshops. Rebecca Becker generously directed students in my original trilogy of one-acts, *Old Wives Tales*. I collaborated during my academic tenure with gifted artists who have created wonderful projects and won many honors in theatre, film and television in the decades since we were young together. Thank you, my Northwestern University family, especially David Downs and those who championed student playwrights.

In Chicago Jeff Ortmann hired me as dramaturg at Wisdom Bridge, where I learned from Richard E. T. White and Christine Sumption. Sandy Shinner invited me to assist her as dramaturg at Victory Gardens. Former Northwestern student Sally Nemeth enlisted me in creating a collective with some of the best writers in town—Chicago New Plays Festival—in which I participated as a dramaturg. Sally continues to inspire and support me. Under the auspices of the Goodman Theatre, with Steve Scott I ventured to Stateville Prison, a men's maximum security facility, for playwriting workshops. Through these activities I made relationships with other dramaturgs in Chicago (thank you, Richard Pettengill) and elsewhere. I truly appreciate all you taught and shared with me, Chicago friends.

In Los Angeles I continued involvement with original plays and writers as a member of the Echo Theatre's collective, thanks again to Sally Nemeth and with special appreciation for director Chris Fields. Donna Rifkind included me in her writers group, a circle of exceptionally talented women who graciously allowed me into their rich imaginative worlds. Collaborating with gifted writer and Northwestern alumnus Steve Totland taught me new skills. For many years in Los Angeles I critiqued plays, screenplays, teleplays and books for film and television producers, which broadened my grasp of dramatic structure immensely. Thank you Kate Benton Doughan (NU again) for making the call that got me into that work and many others who supported my critiques and writing over the years.

Al Watt asked me to teach the 90-Day Play workshop for his L.A. Writers' Lab Workshop on NU alum Allison Burnett's recommendation. That in turn gave me the opportunity and inspiration to create this book. Writers Sally Nemeth, Ariel Shepherd-Oppenheim and Steve Totland have been invaluable as readers for this project. Photographer Suzanne

Plunkett graciously prepared my picture of the Theatre of Dionysus for publication.

My son Robert Jenkins deserves gratitude also for the time I spent in rehearsals and workshops when he was young. And I must thank my mother, Alice Walsh, for her faith in me, and for giving me life and the time I needed to write this book. Through my years in academia and beyond the late Professor Helen Krich Chinoy of Smith College was an invaluable and beloved mentor. Helen modeled professional excellence and nourished me intellectually. Together we published three editions of *Women in American Theatre* (Crown Publishers and then Theatre Communications Group), each edition incorporating new scholarship.

Now *The 90-Day Play* is in your hands and I thank you for the opportunity to share my love of playwriting anew.

Author overlooking Theatre of Dionysus in Athens.

Made in the USA
San Bernardino, CA
21 November 2017